DIAGNOSIS:
HUMAN

THE MENTAL HEALTH SYSTEM
AS A PORTAL TO THE
COLLECTIVE PSYCHE

LINDSEY CARTER, LCSW

TABLE OF CONTENTS

Introduction

It's time to expand the collective consciousness around mental health, and I felt called to offer an elevated perspective. To shine a light on what is, so we can imagine what can be. To bring clarity and cohesion to areas of confusion. To create a little form and structure from the nebulous.

We've somehow allowed things to get out of hand and are now looking to the mental health system and its primary text, the *Diagnostic and Statistical Manual of Mental Disorders*, Fifth Edition (DSM-5) to tell us who we are and who we should be. In outsourcing our personal power to the system, we've entered into a trauma bond with it.

The belief that we are broken and in need of an outside authority figure to fix or rescue us is the societal core wound that I feel is responsible for our dependency on the mental health system.

The good news is that we are already beginning to heal and transmute this wound simply by observing it. The willingness to explore our relationship to the mental health system is the first step toward empowerment and sovereignty. Only then can we take what it is showing us about ourselves and use it to access true, sustainable healing, embody our wholeness, and create a gentler reality.

See below for a few of the topics I cover in this book:

- Inherent conflicts of interest within the therapist job description
- The ways in which therapists' personal trauma and wounding impact the way they relate to clients
- How the therapist–client relationship often mirrors a parent-child relationship (potentially a dysfunctional or abusive one)

- How therapists and clients are positioned as adversaries
- The ways therapists' education and training fail to equip them to comprehensively assess clients
- The shortcomings in the diagnostic criteria and process, including the inability to achieve standardization and ensure accuracy
- How the usage of psychiatric medications can act as a barrier to determining the root cause of health concerns
- Misogyny and misandry in the mental health system
- A critical analysis of the authority the mental health system has been given, as well as thoughts on depedastalizing it in our hearts and minds
- An exploration of the mental health system as a microcosm of society and of our individual internal state
- How exploring our relationship with the system can help us see where we're outsourcing our personal power
- Thoughts on healing ourselves and our world

In this book, I explore the ways the mental health system capitalizes on our collective soul loss and how our desire for self-knowledge and well-being are weaponized against us. I draw from my twelve years of experience working in the mental health field and my own healing journey to share some of the lesser-known aspects of the clinical therapeutic setting and the limitations of the mental health system and diagnostic criteria.

Why I Chose to Write This Book

Following an acute traumatic event in 2020 and a subsequent Lyme disease flare-up, I had the eye-opening experience of being unable to access the support I needed for my own healing within the mental health system. During this time, I realized that the system actually has very little to offer people whose concerns fall too far outside the box, and that the general public doesn't seem to be aware of this. This is really concerning, considering the mental health system is one of the major underpinnings of our society.

When I use the term *underpinning*, I'm referring to a shared mental construct that is foundational to the way we perceive ourselves and our world. Over time, these constructs become so deeply ingrained into the hive mind, or collective consciousness, that they run unquestioned in the background, informing our day-to-day reality from behind the scenes. The actual underpinning is the ideology surrounding the mental health system, as opposed to the physical system itself (mental health facilities, practitioners, etc.). I refer to this as the Mental Health *Belief* System (MHBS).

A few core tenets of the MHBS are:

- There is a right and wrong way to be.
- We require explicit guidelines to define right and wrong, as well as someone outside ourselves to tell us which category we fall into.
- To receive help for mental and emotional concerns, we must first be assigned a label.
- People who navigate life differently than what is considered normal are disordered.
- Someone either has a mental health condition or they don't (instead of understanding that mental and emotional concerns exist on a continuum).
- It is actually possible to define the totality of the human experience.
- The human experience can be adequately conveyed in a written text.

The Mental Health Belief System is sustaining the mental health system and *is being sustained by it.*

Said another way:

The mental health system mirrors back to us—and thus reinforces—the beliefs that created it, making it somewhat of a vicious cycle at this point.

When viewed through this lens, it's easy to see how members of a society where the MHBS is the dominant narrative get caught in the crossfire. Most of us were highly conditioned—if not completely indoctrinated—to buy into the MHBS ideology from a very young age. We accepted the beliefs as absolute truth because we didn't know any better, and now we aren't really sure what life would look like without them.

The way I see it, the majority of the population is in a relationship with the mental health system, by way of the MHBS. To test this theory, I considered the percentage of the population who have never engaged directly with the system in any way. They haven't seen a therapist, been assessed for admission to an inpatient psychiatric facility, or discussed mental or emotional concerns with their primary care doctor. There is still a high likelihood they subscribe to many of the beliefs that make up the MHBS due to how prevalent and deeply ingrained the MHBS ideology is in our society.

One may assume that such widespread ideological conformity would result in increased knowledge and understanding of the mental health system; however, I have not found that to be the case. While I do believe the general public is beginning to question various aspects of the mental health system, many people still appear intimidated, confused, or even scared of it. Because of this, it has managed to slip under the radar and avoid scrutiny. I also find it interesting that while several psychiatrists and psychologists have spoken out about the harmful aspects of the mental health system, I'm not aware of therapists doing the same. This is another reason I felt compelled to share my perspective.

Because mental health professionals are working with people in vulnerable states and making decisions that affect their lives, there should be no trade secrets.

True informed consent can only occur in the presence of full transparency.

A Brief Disclaimer

Part of my journey has been fully allowing myself to explore the shadow side of all the major systems in the US. I wanted to know the good, the bad, the ugly, and everything in between. This includes the medical and mental health systems, the political arena, the military, the legal system, organized religion, the financial system, and academia. What these systems all have in common is a pretty dark history, being profit driven, containing some element of a power-over dynamic, and a tendency to place the needs of the system over the people.

The mental health system struck me as particularly inhumane, as its primary text, the DSM-5, is written from an outsider's perspective, instead of the perspective of the person who is actually having the experience. It's like they're observing a human from outside a fish tank, or through metal bars at a zoo. On top of that, it feels like the people who wrote it have never experienced an emotion in their lives, let alone a relationship, a profound loss, or a period of upheaval and transition. Nor do they seem to have navigated a dark night of the soul. I've often wondered if they've ever actually left the office, taken off the suit, and allowed themselves to enter into the messiness of the human experience.

It's the wild, wild West out here!

It takes courage and bravery to allow ourselves to experience life, take risks, get hurt, fail, and then do it all over again; and it just doesn't seem like the people who created the DSM-5 factored that in.

On a Personal Note

At the time of this writing, I am not sure what the future holds for me personally or professionally. I am trusting my inner guidance as I step away from my career in the mental health field and into the unknown. There's a common misconception that to leave something, we have to be against it, and the fact that we're choosing not to participate means we think others should also not participate. That is not the case here. I am choosing what feels right for me and encouraging you to do the same. My goals are simply to inform and share my perspective. It is not my intention to persuade, convince, or coerce you to do anything. I do not have all the answers, nor am I claiming to. I am not your therapist, your mentor, your guru, or your parent.

To write this book, I had to face the parts of myself that still felt like they knew what other people should do. It was vulnerable work, but on the other side of it, I am relieved to proclaim I have no idea what is best for you or anyone else. So please read this with a healthy amount of skepticism, then do your own research. As with anything, take the best and leave the rest!

This book is not medical or mental health advice.

Tips for Readers

To get the most out of this book, I recommend the following:

1.   Let go of the need to draw conclusions or have all the answers.

Focus on just receiving the material for what it is: my perspective. There's no pressure to accept this book as truth, or to take any action whatsoever as a result of reading it.

2.   Take breaks when you need to.

Because of how comprehensive and thorough I tried to be, this book contains a lot of information—some of which may be new. It will likely take time and energy to process what I'm sharing and to reconcile any cognitive dissonance that may arise.

You may want to highlight meaningful phrases, make notes in the margins, and fold down the corners of the pages you want to revisit once you have the big picture.

The chapters of this book are similar to blog entries or mini essays, in that they each address a different topic. This makes it conducive to reading a few chapters then taking time to digest the information before picking it back up. There's no rush. It's not going anywhere!

3.   Don't hesitate to do a little research on your own for more context.

In hopes of having a shared language, I've provided working definitions within the text of terms that may not be widely used in everyday conversation. However, I stuck pretty closely to the way the terms are used in both the mental health field and holistic health settings, so it shouldn't be too hard to find more information if needed.

4.   Take full advantage of the wealth of knowledge that is the appendixes.

They could be their own book on health and healing. I decided to include the information on holistic health because I know how hard it is to loosen our grip on one paradigm without having another one to explore, and because it has the potential to help move the needle for those in a healing process.

I focused on information I wish I'd known a lot earlier in my own journey in hopes of saving people both time and money on theirs.

A Few Notes on How the Information Is Presented

1. **I use the word** *person,* **as opposed to** *therapist* **or** *mental health practitioner,* **several times throughout the book where the role is implied.**

I do this for two reasons:

- **It's a reminder that I'm talking about actual people.**

    Mental health professionals are people first. They do not lose their personhood once they earn a degree or are issued a license. This means they can exhibit the positive traits of being a person, such as generosity, empathy, and compassion, but also that they're capable of being incompetent, negligent, dishonest, and vindictive.

- **To emphasize that the mental health system is composed of people, just like you and me.**

    This is a reminder that it is imperfect, and perhaps even fragile.
    By becoming overly dependent on the medical and mental health systems, we will likely see aspects of them fall. I'm speaking primarily to our perception of what these structures have to offer us when I use the word *fall,* but it could take on many forms.

2. **When I use the term** *organized religion,* **I am speaking to the man-made components of faith and spirituality.**

Rather than to engage directly with specific ideologies, my intention with this book is to assist you in becoming healthier and more empowered so that you can make conscious decisions in all aspects of your life—including religion and spirituality.

The way we do something matters, so the ability to engage with ideologies or belief systems from a place of wholeness can make all the difference!

Having religious or spiritual beliefs is not required to benefit from this book.

Chapter 1

My Story

In the summer of 2021, I took a break from practicing as a therapist after a series of challenging life events. The first one was receiving a diagnosis of Lyme disease in 2019, followed by a military discharge a few months later, then an acute traumatic event in March of 2020.

Fast-forward to 2023. I was feeling better and was ready to get back to work. However, despite the long break, I still had so much resistance to transferring my license to Florida and calling myself a therapist again. I couldn't quite put my finger on why this was, so I kept hoping I could make it work. After going back and forth for months and "trying" several times to complete the licensure paperwork and set up my business structure (which I now see were halfhearted attempts), I decided in February 2024 that the mental health field just wasn't for me.

As with most big transitions in my life, the decision to no longer practice as a therapist was both gradual and abrupt. On some level, I'd known for a while, but it was still an extremely hard decision to make after being so invested in my career for over twelve years at that point.

For those who appreciate a little context and a timeline: I graduated from Harding University in Searcy, Arkansas, in 2009 with a bachelor's degree in social work, then attended the University of South Carolina's Master of Social Work program in Columbia, South Carolina. My graduate school internship was at Fort Jackson Army post, where I worked with active-duty soldiers in the mental health clinic, as well as basic trainees as they completed in-processing and began their integration into the military training environment. I performed mental health evaluations for drill sergeants, led support groups for injured soldiers, sat in on meetings with the clinical staff at Moncrief Army Health Clinic, and even attended a yoga and mindfulness class for soldiers experiencing symptoms associated with post-traumatic stress disorder (PTSD).

Following grad school, I was hired as a hospice social worker in the fall of 2010 at the age of twenty-three. I worked alongside palliative care nurses, nursing assistants, chaplains, and volunteers to support patients who were nearing the end of their lives. This included making routine visits to the patients' homes (including nursing homes and assisted living facilities) and providing assistance with advance directives, funeral planning, caregiver support, connection to community resources, and nursing home placement.

In 2013, I direct commissioned into the Army National Guard and served as my state's first full-time behavioral health officer from 2014 to 2017, working alongside medical providers to ensure service members were mentally fit for military service (both stateside and during deployment). Together, we created the state's first mental health program and established mental health policies and procedures to be implemented statewide (approximately nine thousand soldiers). My primary responsibility as a full-time behavioral health officer (BHO) was to oversee the mental health clinical team, including civilian case managers, enlisted soldiers (usually combat medics), and the part-time BHOs who joined us once a month on drill weekends.

I resigned from active duty in 2017 to go into private practice as a therapist. I wanted to provide mental health treatment, which I was not able to do in my position with the National Guard. In the late summer of 2017, I completed training in EMDR (Eye Movement Desensitization and Reprocessing), which is a type of trauma therapy that uses bilateral stimulation, such as eye movements, tapping, or auditory tones, to help the brain reprocess traumatic memories. I used EMDR alongside other therapeutic techniques to treat clients experiencing symptoms associated with depression, anxiety, post-traumatic stress disorder (PTSD), obsessive-compulsive disorder (OCD), attention deficit hyperactivity disorder (ADHD), and insomnia. Throughout my career, I was also actively involved in equipping the next generation of social workers by supervising interns and teaching a master's-level social work course at the University of South Carolina as adjunct faculty.

Although being a social worker wasn't always easy, I enjoyed it and did everything I could to be effective in my various roles. Looking back, I would say my career was the perfect combination of adventurous, challenging, fascinating, heart-breaking, stressful, and ultimately rewarding. I wouldn't trade one minute of it. While I encountered a few systemic challenges over the years, it was pretty easy to write them off as specific to the job position, office climate, or bureaucratic BS you often find in government agencies and organizations. It wasn't until I had my own intense healing crisis—and subsequent awakening—that I saw the full extent of the situation and realized something is just fundamentally wrong with the way mental health is being addressed in the US.

The catalyst for my awakening was a life-altering event in early 2020 that affected my living situation, resulted in a Lyme disease flare-up, and caused repressed childhood memories to surface. It was a distressing interaction with someone who had been in my life for a long time. I was staying with them for a few weeks while looking for an apartment in Nashville. The interaction began with me asking a question, then quickly escalated. They became very aggressive and said extremely hurtful and shocking things about who I was as a person, and the life I'd created. To make it worse, I'd only planned to stay with this person for a week or two, but it turned into a little longer due to very destructive tornadoes hitting Nashville on March 3, then the news of the pandemic slowly trickling into Middle Tennessee. Basically, I'd gotten stuck.

I've always told therapy clients that we don't get to choose what constitutes as traumatic for our minds and bodies, and that was certainly the case here. Despite the event not being a physical altercation, it seemed to register that way in my system, as the person was much larger than me and was very upset.

Following the event, I was extremely dysregulated for over a year. It felt like my nervous system was completely shot. I was exhausted, but I could not rest. The constant hypervigilance significantly worsened the physical symptoms I had prior to 2020 (chemical sensitivities, brain fog, food intolerances, etc.). Because Nashville was so chaotic following the tornadoes and news of the pandemic, I wasn't sure I wanted to stay there. Since I wasn't in a lease and had already moved my work online, I decided that my guinea pig and I would pack up the SUV and travel for a few months to get clarity on what to do with our lives. I also hoped we could reestablish a sense of safety in our bodies and in the world, but apparently that was too much to ask considering the current state of affairs. I tried to pretend we were on an adventure, but in retrospect, it was a disaster—second only to the one occurring on the world stage! If it hadn't been for Piggy and the sense of responsibility I felt for keeping her safe and finding us a new home, I don't know what I would've done.

Although we visited some of my all-time favorite spots, such as Charleston, South Carolina; Asheville, North Carolina; and Destin, Florida—as well as my former home of several years, Columbia, South Carolina—our travel adventures were far from ideal. I had the worst case of PTSD I'd ever seen (or at least the most acute case), and while I tried to enjoy the scenery, I couldn't help but feel like I was barely winning the race to outrun my problems, and that it would all catch up to me very soon.

I remember trying to sleep one night and having the sensation that the darkness was choking me, which made it impossible to wear my usual earplugs and eye mask. I was barely sleeping at all, and my brain's executive functioning was basically nonexistent. Because executive functioning includes time management and completing tasks, it was nearly impossible to plan anything, including where to stay the next night—much less the next week or month! By the fall of that year, I had gained over fifteen pounds (despite having an extremely clean diet and low appetite), lost half my hair, and was experiencing anxiety and restlessness like never before. Basically, my goal during that time was to just keep moving until I couldn't anymore—which, to an extent, is the way I'd lived my life prior to the traumatic event, so in some ways it felt normal (albeit amplified).

Onward and Upward for Me, But Not Quite Yet!

I finally found a spot to land (crash into) in August 2020. It was a partially converted office space in Black Mountain, North Carolina, right outside Asheville. While I'd been to Asheville several times, Black Mountain was new to me. The listing caught my eye because the building was EMF mitigated. EMF stands for electromagnetic fields, which are produced by any device that uses electricity, but especially cell phones, Wi-Fi routers, electric meters, and power lines. Because I'd become extremely sensitive to EMF over the past few years, I was pleasantly surprised to see the listing—even if it was a little unconventional in that it still had a commercial or business vibe, as opposed to residential.

Following a quick trip to Black Mountain to see the space, and getting the official thumbs-up from Piggy, I decided it was just as good as anywhere else, and coordinated with the landlord on a move-in date. I chose the actual office part to be my bedroom, and what looked to be the staff break room as my kitchen/office. A plug-in stove burner and a refrigerator were provided, and I purchased a $300 portable washing machine from Home Depot. I found a used desk and a couple of room divider screens on Facebook Marketplace, then just tried to make the most of the situation. The arrangement wasn't without its challenges, but at least it offered some stability and seemed to be a good place to hide out for a while, cry, and get some rest; but alas, only the middle one would prove to be true.

Piggy died two weeks after we arrived in North Carolina, and I buried her in the courtyard at three a.m. by the light of my cell phone. She had gotten sick before we left Nashville and was very resistant to the medication regimen, but I'd been holding out hope she would pull through.

I considered leaving this part out, but Piggy was a main character in my life and will no longer be part of the story, so I figured an explanation was in order. Dedicating one small paragraph to her is the least I can do after dragging her around the whole southeastern corner of the US on my self-discovery road trip!

Around this time, distressing childhood memories began to surface. Because my body had already been through so much, it seemed to lack the infrastructure or scaffolding to hold such intensity, and I started "bottoming out." That was the only way I could describe the nightly panic attacks, during which I would jolt awake and not know who I was or where I was. I told a friend that I was "taking the elevator straight down to hell" every night, nearly without exception.

I was also experiencing frequent emotional flashbacks. Similar to panic attacks, emotional flashbacks are periods of emotional intensity (terror, dread, hopelessness, panic) accompanied by body sensations of a traumatic event. They often have no memory attached. I intuitively knew I was releasing the trauma and that it was temporary; however, I can understand how people assume that panic attacks and flashbacks will get worse without medical intervention. I'm going to explore in a later chapter where those beliefs may have originated, but for now you can refer to Appendix B to see what I found to be true, along with some tools that helped me cope with the stress of that time.

Personal Share

As you'll see throughout the book, I am not one to overidentify with diagnostic labels for mental or physical health, because I often feel they are overly simplified and do not take into account the mind-body-spirit connection or the totality of the person. This includes Lyme disease and MCAS (mast cell activation syndrome). However, I use these terms in an attempt to provide a shared language. The irony is that both Lyme and MCAS present differently in everyone, so it can still be hard to get a clear picture of people's experiences, even when using the terms.

It may also be helpful to know that both Lyme and MCAS are systemic, in that they can affect any and all body systems. They are exacerbated by stress (emotional, chemical, physical, or mental), and it's not unusual for those who experience Lyme and MCAS to have other co-occurring conditions, as well as a history of childhood trauma.

There is a lot of confusion, and even controversy, surrounding Lyme disease—including where it originated, how it's transmitted, and how to test for it—all of which is outside the scope of this book. However, the general consensus is that we contract it from a tick bite and that, if caught in time, an antibiotic can treat current symptoms and prevent future ones. Because I'd already been experiencing symptoms for several years prior to seeing a Lyme-literate medical doctor (LLMD) in 2019, that wasn't an option.

Since I was making progress with my functional medicine doctor (FMD) in Nashville, the recommendation was to continue working with him and to manage stress more effectively. This was fine with me, as my primary goal for seeing him was to explore the possibility of Lyme, even if that meant ruling it out. It was clear to me (even prior to the event in 2020) that my body had reached a tipping point and needed support, and that taking medication would only serve as a temporary solution at best.

During the fall of 2020, I was still working remotely with my FMD, but I struggled to articulate what I was experiencing. It was so hard to know what to focus on when it seemed like everything was wrong. In addition to feeling completely overwhelmed, I was also having trouble formulating words when I tried to discuss anything related to the traumatic event. I didn't realize until a year later during a call with my FMD that I never actually told him what happened. I basically talked around it for a whole year and he just went with the program!

At some point, I noticed that my memories and dreams had switched to the third person, as if I was watching myself on a movie screen. I also did not recognize my face in the mirror. I knew it was me, of course, but there wasn't the *felt sense* of it being me. It wasn't that I actually looked that different either. It was that the brain region that governed facial recognition had seemingly gone offline. In retrospect, I believe my brain and body were trying to protect me by splitting off like that. The underlying message seemed to be something along the lines of "It's not safe to be a self" or even "It's not safe to be me."

As far as general life functioning, I was dipping in and out of shock and confusion to the point of having to reorient myself when I drove from the gas station to the grocery store.

Ugh! You couldn't pay me to go back to that time.

I learned at some point that these can all be symptoms of brain inflammation, which explains why the inside of my head felt physically hot in the evenings. Following lab work and some functional medicine tests, my FMD formulated a supplement protocol to support my mind and body. However, when you're doing that terribly, nothing works fast enough, and even trying to function in your day-to-day life is traumatizing and retraumatizing over and over again. It's not that we hadn't tried making a plan prior to that, but I was too dysregulated to implement a regimen of any kind. Plus, I didn't have a permanent address to ship the supplements to.

This may be a good time to share that there was absolutely a spiritual component to this part of my journey. After all, if not recognizing your own face isn't an invitation to connect with yourself and higher guidance at an even deeper level, I don't know what is! I share more about that aspect in Chapter 31, but I just wanted to briefly acknowledge it here.

Anyway, because of everything going on, I figured I should find a therapist to at least sit there while I tried to make sense of my life. The goal was to find one who offered something other than talk therapy, such as EMDR or Brainspotting. Because of the way these modalities engage directly with the brain and nervous system to resolve trauma, they tend to be more effective than talk therapy alone. Unfortunately, I got quite an education and sustained even more trauma when I sought help from the mental health system and the practitioners within it. I am not exaggerating when I say I had either a phone consult, an in-person appointment, or a telehealth session with over *eight* therapists in the course of a year and a half before finally giving up. None of them seemed to know what I was talking about, much less have any relevant or valuable feedback to offer. Because I had the same credentials and experience as most of the practitioners I spoke with, I could clearly see how they were limited and where their knowledge base ended. However, I still was not immune to feelings of hopelessness, confusion, and frustration at times over their inability to connect with me.

If you're wondering why I didn't reach out to someone with more credentials, it's because the only other options were doctors—either psychiatrists or psychologists. As a general rule, psychologists focus primarily on psychological testing, and psychiatrists focus on prescribing medication. Since I wasn't seeking either of those options I was left to choose from clinicians at my level (LCSWs, LPCs, and LMFTs). I'll explain more about therapists' education and licensing in Chapter 4.

Anyway, if I had to pick the top three areas where there seemed to be a breakdown in communication and understanding with the therapists I saw, they would be the following:

- **A lack of knowledge of Lyme disease and other physical health concerns that can affect someone's mental health.**
  There did not seem to be an understanding that physical health concerns can present as mental health symptoms (due to systemic inflammation, toxicity, etc).

- **A deficit in their own life experience or personal healing.**
  It was hard to know what was going on here. I just know that when I shared what I was experiencing I was met with a blank stare.

- **A lack of diversity, variation, or depth in their clinical experience.**
  Once again, it's hard to know where the disconnect was, but the therapists did not seem to have any frame of reference for what I was going through. It was as if I was the most severe case they'd ever seen. Although I was really struggling, I still made it to appointments on time and communicated clearly, so I'm not sure what the problem was.

For these reasons, I could not trust or respect these therapists (clinically or otherwise), and I didn't feel comfortable seeing them for therapy. If I'm being honest, I started to ask myself, "What are they even for?" and "Why should I listen to them?" Since we had the same education and licensing, the question that surfaced most often was "What sets them apart from me?" People who don't work in the mental field may hold the education and licensing in very high esteem, but what good was it actually doing at this point? All things being equal, I seemed to know just as much as (if not more than) they did.

Another interesting dynamic I observed—although I could not process or articulate it at the time—can only be described as a sense of superiority from the therapists. Now, this could totally be my own projection, but I really don't think it was. Instead of compassion and empathy, the emotion I felt from them was pity. There also seemed to be a lack of awareness that it could just as easily be them in my position. That I was them.

That *I am them.*

We're all human, and at the end of the day, no one is immune to the challenges and hardships of the human experience.

Mental health professionals often go into the field specifically to avoid facing life and being vulnerable, so to be met with a reminder that all the academic degrees, licenses, certifications, and trainings only offer the *illusion* of safety rather than *actual* safety was probably very unsettling. It was for me too! I think the idea that the credentials and professional achievements only get us so far—or that we can't hide behind them forever—is potentially destabilizing for most people.

At the present time, I live with the acute awareness that we're all just one EVENT away from a drastically different life, and from potentially needing a lot of help. This knowledge can be heavy at times, and it has certainly changed the way I engage with the world. While I'm not going to brag about how much humility I have now, I will say that I'm able to access exponentially more compassion and empathy for people, and that I now perceive much less separation between myself and others.

Running parallel to my own intense healing journey was my professional disillusionment with basically the whole thing. After all, if I couldn't get the help I needed, then what hope is there for people with less knowledge of mental health, or those with fewer resources? Because I'd worked in the mental health field since my early twenties, I had an idea of what options were out there. I also had personal and professional contacts I could reach out to if needed. However, even with all of those things, I still wasn't finding the answers I was looking for. I started asking myself questions, such as "What do people who have no experience with personal growth and healing do?" and "What about those who aren't very self-aware or who struggle to articulate what they're going through?"

In retrospect, I was realizing that the emperor had no clothes. Other than a few healing modalities that the mental health system holds hostage, it didn't have very much to offer. Let's just say it was all very humbling, to say the least.

During this time, I began to critically and thoroughly question everything I thought I knew about the mental health system. The goal was to get clarity on exactly "what is happening" (actual quote from my internal dialogue at the time) before making any decisions about the future of my career as a mental health professional. I was trying to determine whether it was possible to show up as my true self and still affect positive change within the parameters of the current system, or if continuing to practice as a therapist would require me to forfeit my authenticity and compromise on my principles.

Chapter 2

Clarifying Our Goals for Mental and Emotional Health

Before beginning to write this book, I posted the following question on my social media page:

> When you seek support from the mental health system, what are you hoping to gain?
>
> A. To have someone to talk to
>
> B. A diagnosis or clarity around a previous diagnosis
>
> C. Medication
>
> D. To determine whether you're "normal"
>
> E. To function more effectively in your life (organization, time management, prioritizing tasks)
>
> F. A sense of inner peace and well-being
>
> G. To improve your relationships
>
> H. To access benefits or resources
>
> I. You feel like you *should* talk to someone—either because you were told you should, or you feel your symptoms are so severe that you need to be monitored by a professional

I received only two responses to my informal little poll!

However, following multiple conversations with friends, former therapists, and practitioners of other healing modalities, I came to the conclusion that many people actually have no idea what they're looking for when reaching out to a mental health professional.

It seems like everyone wants to feel "better," but there isn't a shared definition of what "better" actually means. It's highly individualized and depends on where you are and where you want to be. I realized while writing this book that the words *health* and *well-being* are also highly subjective.

The good news is you get to choose what health and well-being mean for you and how to utilize your available resources to experience them.

For the purposes of this chapter, your specific goals for mental and emotional health are less important than learning how to determine whether the practitioner you're working with can assist you in reaching them. I can think of few things more discouraging than getting several months into a healing process with a practitioner before realizing they are operating according to an entirely different paradigm or map. This is the equivalent of setting out on a cross-country road trip with a friend and discovering after several hours that they're driving toward Albuquerque, New Mexico, when you thought you were on your way to Atlanta, Georgia to see a Braves game! The way this can look in the mental health system is a therapist defining well-being as symptom management by lifelong therapy, medication, or both. If this is not something you're interested in then that practitioner—or treatment framework—may not be the one for you.

Over the past few years, I've heard countless stories of people feeling disappointed and underwhelmed by their experiences with the mental health system and realizing at some point that in order to truly heal, they need to explore options outside of it. I feel pretty safe in saying that when this happens, they rarely—if ever—contact their former therapist to give an update on their status or to share what helped them. Because of this, mental health professionals may be operating at a deficit when it comes to data on outcomes. They're only seeing what it looks like when a client stays in treatment, as opposed to where the other roads lead. It's as if they're only seeing the first half of the movie.

This is not an attack on therapists, as I do believe most are well-meaning. It is quite possible that they're being very honest when they tell clients that their condition is incurable, the prognosis is poor, or that they will require medication for the duration of their life. Once again, this outcome may be all the practitioner has seen and what they believe to be true. It's just a reminder that they are limited in some ways. This is why it's in your best interest to do your own research, and to not be afraid to seek out other resources when trying to heal, instead of looking to mental health professionals to be the all-knowing gurus.

Questions to consider when deciding who to partner with to address your mental and emotional health:

1. How do I want my life to be different?
2. How will I know when it's changed?
3. Can the person I'm working with help me achieve my goals?
4. Do they have a road map of where I want to go?
5. Have they helped others get there?
6. Have they been there themselves?

Chapter 3
Pressure to Seek Mental Health Treatment

The pendulum has swung. The stigma around seeking treatment has turned into a stigma around not seeking it.

When I started my private practice in Nashville in 2018, I noticed a trend: Having a therapist had become the cool, new, sexy thing, especially among the college crowd. They loved nothing more than quoting their therapist in conversations with friends and family or making a short video about what they were learning in therapy, then posting it on social media.

While sharing quotes and videos can be a lot of fun, it can also contribute to the idea that everyone *should* be in therapy—and even a sense of superiority over those who aren't. While it makes sense that people would be eager to share about mental health therapy if they've found it to be beneficial, it's another thing entirely to assume therapy would be equally helpful for everyone.

> **Due to such extreme variation in people's experiences with therapy and therapeutic outcomes, I personally question the belief that engagement with the mental health system is an automatic indicator that someone is healthier or more evolved than anyone else.**

Let me explain. Healing isn't a linear trajectory, and the different approaches to healing cannot be organized into a hierarchy. For example, some people may see a therapist for years but make more progress at a two-week retreat in Peru working with a shaman than they did in hundreds of clinical therapy sessions. However, there may also be people who spend years traveling to other countries and exploring various spiritual teachings and healing practices, who eventually find therapy was the missing piece for them.

Related to the idea that healing can take many different forms, I want to add that the mental health system (inpatient or outpatient) is not necessarily a higher level of care. For example, there's a belief that if a person's mental health symptoms are too severe, the *only* option is to be evaluated and potentially admitted into an inpatient psychiatric facility. In reality, the best course of action depends on multiple factors, such as the person's resources, health goals, and whether they require medical stabilization (often the case with substance addiction, withdrawal, or overdose).

In order for an inpatient facility to be a higher level of care, it needs to offer something better than what the person has available outside of it.

Oftentimes, inpatient psychiatric stays are far more traumatizing than the original trauma that resulted in the admission to begin with, so there's a lot to consider. To my knowledge, most psychiatric facilities rely on medication as a primary means of stabilization. Some may try to incorporate individual and group therapy but are limited by insurance requirements and staffing shortages. My hope is that different options will become available as we learn what our bodies actually need to be well, and how to proactively care for ourselves so we don't end up in a crisis to begin with.

Unfortunately, many people struggle daily with mental health symptoms. It is not unusual for them to be told by a medical practitioner that they must engage in weekly outpatient therapy sessions, in addition to being overseen by a doctor for medication management. While this may be helpful for some, I've known plenty of people who decided they did not want to do this for the rest of their lives, and decided instead to make lifestyle changes that contributed to improved mental and emotional health. It seemed the most common areas addressed were relationships, career, diet, activity level, and living situations.

While I'm not trying to discourage anyone from reaching out for help or support, it's important to get really clear on what is actually helpful and supportive.

So, back to the pendulum swing and the idea that everyone should be engaged in mental health treatment. . .

We can all probably think of someone who we wish would get help for their mental and emotional health. We may even feel justified in telling them what kind of help it should be, along with how all our lives would improve immediately if they would just take our advice. However, the decision to engage in personal healing work is exactly that—personal; and the person in question may not have any interest. They may be fine at their current level of functioning. However, there's also a possibility that the type of help they're being offered doesn't feel helpful.

For the reasons mentioned above, the clinical mental health setting is not for everyone, and that is okay! Whether it's because of trauma or God-given intuition, a no is a no, and it doesn't matter why.

There is no shame in seeking support elsewhere. Just because the mental health system still seems to be the automatic go-to in some circles, it doesn't mean it's a great fit for everyone. Some people choose to heal using holistic modalities, like meditation, yoga, physical detox and cleansing, acupuncture, and sound healing. All of these have different benefits, so it just depends on the person's goals.

Let's normalize healing in whatever way works, no matter how unconventional it may seem.

I'll share more about what helped me heal in Chapter 37.

A few reminders about mental health treatment:

- Only you can decide what healing looks like for you.
- You have the right to discontinue a treatment at any time (although I recommend doing it gradually and safely).
- You have the right to not seek any treatment at all.

Chapter 4
Foundational Information on the Mental Health System

Before we get too far into the material, I'd like to provide a very basic overview of the mental health system, including its practitioners and the various clinical settings they operate in.

The following terms can be used interchangeably to mean anyone who holds a medical or mental health license and works with people to address their mental health concerns:

- Professional
- Practitioner
- Provider
- Clinician

There are many different types of practitioners in the mental health system, but I primarily focus on therapists for the majority of this book, unless otherwise stated.

Licensure

There are several different educational paths therapists can take, as well as a few different types of licensure. However, all independently licensed therapists are authorized to assign mental health diagnostic labels and treat mental health concerns without a doctor's supervision.

A few examples of the different credentials are the following:

- **LISW-CP:** Licensed Independent Social Worker-Clinical Practice
- **LCSW:** Licensed Clinical Social Worker
- **LMFT:** Licensed Marriage and Family Therapist
- **LPC:** Licensed Professional Counselor

Practice Settings

While therapists may work in a variety of clinical settings, my primary focus is in the outpatient private practice setting. Therapists in private practice typically see clients for individual therapy for fifty minutes every week or every other week, depending on the client's presentation and goals. Therapy sessions are often decreased or scheduled further apart as clients make progress.

A client or patient is anyone who completes the mental health provider's intake paperwork (particularly the Consent to Treat form) and engages in either inpatient or outpatient mental health treatment in the form of individual or group sessions. Individuals who see a therapist in an outpatient or office setting are referred to as clients, while those who are admitted to an inpatient mental health facility, a hospital psychiatric unit, or a residential treatment program are typically referred to as patients. The majority of the time, mental health treatment is voluntary. However, there are cases when treatment is court ordered or individuals are admitted involuntarily. This is usually due to them being deemed a danger to themselves or others.

Therapists working in both outpatient and inpatient settings are required to abide by their respective Code of Ethics, which sets standards for professional boundaries and communication. This is in addition to the policies and procedures of their specific workplace.

Professional Communication

There are three main components of professional communication in the therapeutic setting:

1. Clinically relevant conversation topics

Discussions with clients should pertain to the client's goals for treatment and the focus of the therapy session. There are slight exceptions, such as small talk when opening or closing a session, and unplanned interactions that occur in the community. An example of an unplanned interaction is the therapist and client seeing each other at the grocery store or a little league baseball game.

2. Intentional use of self-disclosure

Therapists are taught to be very careful when deciding what personal information to share with clients. Self-disclosure is to be used intentionally and skillfully to relate to the client and build trust and rapport.

3. Using discernment when making recommendations to clients

Therapists can be held responsible for negative outcomes resulting from advice they give to clients. Because therapists are licensed, the guidance they give to clients is seen as a clinical recommendation. This includes financial, legal, and health advice, as well as information on healing modalities, etc.

It's important for therapists to stay within their area of expertise and avoid recommending anything that could cause harm. I'm aware that this term is vague, and I will explain more soon. This topic is very tricky. Although a therapist may have extensive knowledge on a wide variety of subject matters, it's not necessarily appropriate to share everything they know with clients.

The above list not only applies to therapy sessions, but also to communication outside of the session, such as phone and email correspondence. Healthy communication and boundaries help create a safe container for the client's healing work. It is for this reason that therapists can face disciplinary action for failing to practice professional communication and boundaries.

Code of Ethics and Investigations

Therapists have a Code of Ethics that outlines what is expected of them and sets forth guidelines on what constitutes ethical mental health practice. Because therapists are overseen by a licensing board, there is always the chance they will be asked to account for their words and actions. This usually takes place in a formal investigation and subsequent hearing when someone files a complaint with the state's licensing board. When this happens, the therapist is asked to put what they said or did into context, explain where they were operating from, and provide the board with insight into their intentions. Following the board's review, a decision will be made about whether the therapist will face disciplinary action.

Investigations into mental health practitioners' misconduct are public knowledge, and the outcomes can be found on the licensing board's website. However, because the state boards differ in how much information they share, many of the websites aren't very specific. For example, if a website shows only a "yes" or "no" regarding disciplinary action, along with license status (active or inactive), it's impossible to know why the therapist was investigated. This means a therapist who engaged in sexual relations with a client is labeled the same as one who paid a client to house-sit while they went on vacation. I'm assuming if the offense is both severe enough *and* proven, the therapist's license would be revoked. However, what constitutes "severe enough," and who are the people deciding? Once again, there's just so much we can't know.

Another factor to consider is how long an investigative process takes. If I had to guess, I'd say it takes six to nine months for the board to arrive at a conclusion, assuming they're able to obtain the information they need in a timely manner. Factors that contribute to the length of the investigative process are the following:

- **Correspondence pertaining to investigations is sent via certified mail, so the turnaround times can vary.**
  This is especially true if the board decides to interview former coworkers whose contact information has changed.

- **Depending on the size of the state, the board may only dedicate one or two days per month to hold hearings, review cases, and make determinations.**
  If the board doesn't have all the information in time, the case review will likely be postponed until the following month.

This is significant because it means therapists who are under investigation and may eventually face disciplinary action are still practicing while the board is collecting data and determining how to proceed. This means your therapist could be guilty of misconduct at varying levels of severity at the time they are assessing and diagnosing you. I'm genuinely curious to know if diagnostic labels are reevaluated if the therapist is found to be unfit for any reason when the diagnostic label was assigned. If there is a process in place for this, I'm not aware of it—but I guess clients could always file a complaint to have the diagnosis contested or see a different therapist to get undiagnosed and potentially re-diagnosed.

As far as my personal experience with the investigative process, several years ago I was asked by the board to give a statement pertaining to the conduct of someone I worked with at the time. I believe I was given the option of submitting a written statement, attending in person, or not contributing at all. I decided to attend in person to decrease the chances of being misunderstood or misinterpreted. It was a little anxiety provoking, but I learned so much. While I felt that those particular board members were reasonable and fair and the hearing was conducted professionally, it still wasn't an experience I want to repeat.

Since I started writing this book, I've thought a lot about how the constant threat of an investigation or disciplinary action can impact therapy sessions. This is what I came up with:

- Therapists try to conduct themselves in ways that do not result in a complaint being filed.
- Therapists act to ensure they will fare well (avoid disciplinary action) if they do end up in front of the board.

While I'm sure both of these factors have contributed to clients' experience of safety over the years, a very interesting picture is forming in my mind. It is a standoff in which the therapist and client are positioned as adversaries, with each one holding something above the other's head.

Let me explain. The therapist has the power and authority to assign any diagnostic label they want and to include supporting documentation in the client's chart (no matter how accurate, inaccurate, or unfavorable). If the client questions or disputes it, the therapist can document the following:

- "Failure to accept diagnosis"
- "Noncompliant with treatment plan"
- "Client exhibits poor self-awareness"
- "Client has minimal insight into behaviors that contribute to interpersonal difficulties"

You may need to pause here to ensure you fully grasp the magnitude of what I'm saying. If you're questioning if this can actually happen, I'm here to tell you it can, and it does.

Okay, so now for the other half of the standoff equation: The client can file a complaint at any time. They could even decide to contact the board but continue seeing the therapist for several more sessions to collect more data or build a case against the therapist. It is in this way the therapist is held hostage because, as we've discussed, they're just trying to stay out of the principal's office.

With this as the operating environment in all clinical settings, both client *and* therapist are, on some level, performing or trying to appease the other. They're potentially both in a freeze-and-fawn state during the interaction. Neither one has the freedom to show up to these interactions in an authentic way because of the parameters surrounding the encounter.

(For a full description of the survival behaviors known as fight, flight, freeze, and fawn, see Appendix C.)

Therapist's Limitations

Now that we've covered what an investigation entails and a few of the ways the possibility of being investigated can impact the therapist–client relationship, I'd like to share more on the last item on the list at the very beginning of this section (components of professional communication):

- *Using discernment when making recommendations to clients*

I included this to illustrate the pressure therapists are under when deciding what to share with clients. If a therapist discusses or recommends anything that the board members view as dangerous or harmful, it can result in their license being revoked.

This section is less about the investigative process, and more about the board members therapists have to answer to when a complaint is filed.

To my knowledge, licensing boards are composed of people who have spent years working in the mental health field, then chose (or at least agreed) to oversee it. Regardless of whether the Western mental health model is the lens through which the board members view the world, it is the one therapists will be viewed through and evaluated by during an investigation. This means healing practices that aren't research-based or deemed best practice may be frowned upon—or even viewed as irresponsible, reckless, and overtly harmful. If part of you is thinking that this is non-negotiably positive and a surefire way to vet the information that is allowed into the clinical therapeutic setting, I want to play devil's advocate for a second. Because medical research is often funded by pharmaceutical companies, many of the studies are compromised due to conflicts of interests. With this as the operating environment, we need to seriously question how much emphasis to put on phrases like "research based" and "best practice."

Another question that comes to mind is:

At what point does the mental health field lose credibility for relying so heavily on potentially compromised and unethical studies, while simultaneously acting as a gatekeeper for holistic methods?

Because therapists may face disciplinary action for using techniques and interventions that aren't research-based, recognized as best practice, or generally accepted by the medical and mental health system, they may be reluctant to share about holistic healing modalities—even if they know how beneficial they can be or if they've utilized them in their own healing. This is something clients need to be aware of when asking therapists for feedback instead of automatically assuming they'll be granted access to the therapist's entire knowledge base.

Therapists also have their professional reputation to consider. If they're labeled "woo-woo" or too "out there" by colleagues, they may lose credibility and limit their reach. While writing this book, I was asked to give an example of something that would fall into this category. While I do have an example to share, the truth is that it could be anything people aren't educated on or have judgment around. This was especially true in the military, as there seemed to be a preference for doing things the way they had always been done instead of thinking too far outside the box. Being limited by others' mental blocks and perceived barriers was extremely frustrating and felt like a double bind. There was just so much I couldn't say, even if I knew it could be helpful. The more I learned about true, sustainable healing for mental and emotional health, the harder it was to function in both the military and the mental health field. By the end of my career(s), I felt like I was under a gag order.

An example of a resource I did not feel comfortable discussing freely in private practice was the usage of psychedelics for healing purposes. In 2018, I read Michael Pollan's book *How to Change Your Mind* and attended the Arizona Psychedelics Conference in early 2019. Following the conference, I continued my own research and later completed two courses in psychedelic integration coaching. I was also following the clinical trials at Johns Hopkins that studied the use of psilocybin in the treatment of OCD, addiction, and eating disorders. However, at the time, I felt it was too soon to discuss psychedelics with clients. For one, they were still illegal in most parts of the US. This not only impacted accessibility, it may also have contributed to an unfavorable stigma. Even though I was aware of several reputable and safe retreat centers in places like Costa Rica, Peru, and Jamaica, I didn't feel comfortable recommending them. Using psychedelics comes with a risk and I couldn't guarantee clients' safety. I also didn't want to be held responsible for unfavorable outcomes. The fact that I was practicing in South Carolina and Tennessee at the time may have contributed as well. I might have felt more comfortable in a more progressive state due to the belief that I had a larger permission field[1] and would be shown more grace if I ever had to plead my case before the board. I'm aware this is a generalization, and I apologize for throwing my home states under the bus. However, I stand by my assessment 100 percent!

It's important to be aware of therapists' limitations so you can adjust your expectations accordingly. If you're viewing therapists as having up-to-date, working knowledge of *all* the healing resources and expect them to share this

---

1. I first heard the term "permission field" on *Reclamation Radio with Kelly Brogan MD* in her episode titled "The Surprising Reason Childbirth Can Kill a Couple's Eros with Eyla Cuenca," released in May 2023, and I loved it so much that I contacted Eyla and was given permission to use it.

information freely, you may want to examine that belief. It's similar to finding out that game show participants were prepped beforehand or are reading off index cards—or that your insurance agent wins a cruise if he sells a certain number of plans. The information doesn't necessarily mean you forgo engagement altogether, but it can help you make a more informed decision about how to navigate the situation.

Sidenote: I'm so relieved I no longer have to be overly cautious when discussing healing modalities or sharing resources.

I can now speak freely about everything I've learned and experienced without worrying that I'm going to be held responsible for other people's decisions.

Just a reminder, we can't control what other people do, and to believe otherwise is codependent. I find it ironic that a large percentage of therapists' time and efforts are spent helping people heal from codependency, yet it's pervasive throughout the entire system.

Chapter 5
Inherent Conflicts in the Therapist Position

Now that we've covered some background information on the constraints therapists are working within, I would like to share my perspective on the job description of a mental health therapist. Right out of the gate, we could split the job description of a mental health therapist into two distinct functions that can easily conflict with each other:

- **Conducting an assessment and providing a diagnosis.**
  Therapists use the DSM-5 to determine whether the client meets the criteria for the conditions listed.

- **Helping people improve their well-being.**
  Therapists assist clients in improving their emotional state or life functioning.

A conflict could arise if the client disagrees with the diagnosis, or if the therapist decides not to assign a diagnosis. Either outcome can result in a client feeling misunderstood, invalidated, or resentful. This could interfere with the therapist-client relationship and become a barrier to therapeutic progress.

In the military, we recognized the difference in these two functions and structured our entire mental health program to reflect this understanding. My position was created specifically to oversee soldiers' fitness for duty (FFD), meaning their ability to perform their military job. This included overseas and stateside deployments. I performed FFD evaluations, reviewed soldiers' mental health treatment records, and consulted with their mental health providers to determine whether they were mentally fit to deploy. These tasks fell into the first category above: assessment and diagnostic.

The second category was called soldier care. Because this was an entirely different mission, my state's Army National Guard hired eight civilian therapists to assist soldiers with life stressors, regardless of whether their military job was affected. This included employment, financial concerns, relationship challenges, and mental and emotional resiliency. The civilian therapists were called psychological health coordinators (PHCs). At the time, the National Guard was not authorized to provide mental health treatment (this may have changed), but the PHCs could help soldiers connect with a therapist and other community resources if needed. The position description for the PHCs fell into the second category: helping people improve their well-being.

Separating medical readiness and soldier care (or assessment and diagnostic and life improvement) is one of the rare instances where military medicine may actually be ahead, as the civilian mental health system has yet to make a distinction between the two functions!

Sidenote: The mental health diagnostic criteria is the same for service members and civilians: the DSM-5. However, service members are required to meet the military's Standards of Medical Fitness, as outlined in Army Regulation (AR) 40-501. [2]

Therefore, if soldiers are diagnosed with certain mental health conditions or if their mental health concerns interfere with their ability to perform their military job after one year of treatment, they are deemed unfit for military service and are recommended for discharge.

Eligibility for **benefits** is determined on an individual basis, but as a general rule, if the service member's health concerns are found to be caused or exacerbated by their military service, they may be eligible for benefits.

---

2. "Army Regulation: Record Details for AR 40-501," Army Publishing Directorate, accessed November 6, 2024, https://armypubs.army.mil/ProductMaps/PubForm/Details.aspx?PUB_ ID=1004688.

Chapter 6

The Therapist Job Position as a Role

To be a therapist is to play a role in exchange for money.

It may sound harsh and insensitive, but at a very basic level, that is what is happening. The fact that being a therapist is playing a role is inherently neutral. I was explaining this to someone recently and referenced a 1990s movie, *Runaway Bride*.[3] I pointed out that Julia Roberts didn't really think she was Maggie Carpenter or that Richard Gere was a reporter named Ike, and neither did the audience. The camera crew and others on the set also were not confused as to whether she actually escaped on her wedding day(s). If they couldn't find her, they knew to check the dressing room! She knew she was playing a role, and so did everyone else. She was also getting paid for it. The fact that therapists are doing the same is not bad or good. It just is. The problem arises when one or both parties fail to realize that it's happening.

If the boundaries are unclear, the chances of someone being harmed exponentially increases.

To clarify, I'm not saying therapists don't feel positive feelings for clients or that they don't want them to have a good life and be well. I'm merely pointing out that it is a contractual agreement with a monetary exchange. They are providing a service and are being compensated.

---

3. Gary Marshall, *Runaway Bride* (Touchstone Pictures, Interstate Communications, Lakeshore Entertainment, 1999).

Why It Matters if Therapists Realize They're Playing a Role

The therapists who deny they are playing a role are likely the most dangerous ones out there.

To unconsciously play a role or wear a mask is to be disconnected from our true selves.

If someone isn't in touch with their humanity, they won't have room for yours.

People who are unconsciously playing a role are compromised. Their approval is contingent upon others also playing a role, and I've found there's very little room for error. They will throw you under the bus in a heartbeat due to their allegiance to the system or program.

Sidenote: As adults, we don't actually require people's approval to stay safe—with the exception of abusive relationships—but within the mental health system, approval from a therapist may become a matter of safety due to the power differential and the authority mental health therapists have been given. I will discuss this more in Chapter 9.

Therapists being unaware they're playing a role usually shows up in one of two ways:

1. **They are so overidentified with the therapist role that they don't seem to have an identity outside of it.**

They show up as a therapist or fixer/rescuer in multiple aspects of their life, and they may believe that is the entire truth of who they are. They usually take their job as a mental health professional very seriously and have a deep loyalty to the system.

The easiest example of this is a therapist who relates to people in their personal life the same way they relate to clients. Often, it can look like overfocusing on other people, playing small to avoid being seen, and using the role of helper/healer to avoid doing inner work. If therapists are doing this, the role may not feel like a role. It may feel like it's their entire identity. I would argue that it's still a role but that they're just overidentified with it.

As I mentioned above, therapists who are overblended with the therapist role may have a tendency to overdiagnose. They may also portray clients unfavorably in their visit notes as a CYA (cover your ass) in case they get subpoenaed in a court case. They can do this by using words such as *noncompliant, disengaged,* and *ambivalent* in hopes they will be absolved of any responsibility for poor therapeutic outcomes. Ironically, these exact words often describe a person who is struggling with their mental health but can also be used to discredit them, depending on the intentions and competency of the person reviewing the clinical record.

2. They don't even bother to play the role.

Unlike the therapists I mentioned above who are overblended with their role, these do not play it at all. They may exhibit poor boundaries with clients by relating to them the same way they do their friends, family, and coworkers. This could look like oversharing personal information or inserting their beliefs and opinions into the therapy session. If this is the case, there's a high likelihood that the interactions lack the necessary formalities required to create safety for clients.

Over the years, I've heard all kinds of stories about therapists who operate outside the Code of Ethics or bend the rules when they feel the occasion calls for it. The story is usually some version of them being the "cool" therapist, or is about the rules being outdated and archaic anyway, so no one goes by them.

Sidenote: The way I see it, working in a system where we're unable or unwilling to operate within the guidelines of that system indicates a lack of integrity. People who do this seem content to derive the benefits of affiliation with the system while not actually doing what is being asked of them. This further degrades the system and can result in it being even less safe for clients due to unclear boundaries, guidelines, and expectations.

Practitioners who realize they can no longer abide by the rules and subsequently remove themselves from the clinical therapeutic setting are actually showing more respect for the system, their clients, and themselves than those who continue working within the system under false pretenses.

If practitioners decide they are unable or unwilling to operate within the parameters of the mental health system, trying to change the rules may be a constructive and mutually beneficial course of action. At least then there would be a chance of helping the other practitioners and clients who are feeling equally constricted.

However, as I'm writing this, I'm remembering long days of seeing clients back-to-back, feeling emotionally and physically drained (and simultaneously a little wired), and having to decide between calling a friend, squeezing in a quick workout, or doing a load of laundry in the few remaining hours before just accepting defeat and calling it a day. This is not even to mention completing administrative tasks such as billing, returning phone calls, and staying current with clinical notes and treatment plans. The work seemed never-ending!

The truth is most therapists are operating at capacity and simply do not have the time or energy it would take to make significant and meaningful changes within the system.

When viewed through this lens, the fact that practitioners continue to work in a system that requires them to self-abandon, or that prevents them from implementing what they consider best practice, may not actually be a matter of integrity, as much as it is a matter of *survival*. This is especially true for mental health professionals who have student loans and families to feed.

While I do not have all the answers, I think it's important to describe the situation as I see it, and to acknowledge when people are being backed into a corner and not offered a dignified way forward.

Behind the Scenes

Many therapists operate under a constant fear that they will face disciplinary action or even lose their license, as I discussed in Chapter 4, so the client gets caught in the crossfire. I would say that in the current system, these concerns are legitimate, which can be a significant barrier in the therapist-client relationship. Viewed from this perspective, the therapist is positioned as the parent who wants the client to behave to ensure they stay out of trouble with the licensing board.

To make it even more complex, when reading through the Code of Ethics and individual state guidelines this past year, I was struck by how vague some of the material is. There is a large amount of gray area that seemingly leaves room for therapists' interpretation, with the goal of affording them clinical autonomy. While this may, at first glance, appear freeing, I learned in the military that unclear guidance rarely benefits the person trying to follow the directions. Instead, it gives the authority figure the power to initiate disciplinary action as they see fit. This positions the licensing board as the parent and the therapist as the child who's trying to behave.

Now, to be clear, I'm not suggesting we start an uprising and try to overthrow the licensing board. The board is in place to protect the public from irresponsible or negligent clinicians. It sets a standard of care and vets practitioners. Currently, it may still provide clients with a sense of safety to know that the practitioners in the mental health system meet the requirements for occupying their position and are adhering to a set of guidelines (at least in theory).

Ideally, potential clients would be so connected to themselves and their inner guidance that they could discern who to work with based on that alone—after doing a little research, of course—but the cruel irony is that people often engage in therapy seeking that very thing! It's unfortunate that in the process of trying to connect to ourselves we can get caught in a loop. It's also worth noting that unless you're working in the mental health field, it can be hard to keep track of what all the letters behind clinicians' names mean, along with the various certifications and levels of licensure.

All that to say, I understand why people are drawn to the idea of a one-stop shop to address their mental and emotional concerns . . . if only it were that easy!

Chapter 7

How Mental Health Therapists Differ from Other Health Practitioners

Let's take a closer look at some of the ways mental health therapists are different from other practitioners, starting with the boundaries they're expected to uphold.

The therapist's Code of Ethics states that dual relationships are prohibited. This means it is unethical for therapists to form friendships with clients or interact with them outside the clinical setting. It is also unethical for therapists to provide therapeutic services to people they're already friends with. The therapist–client relationship is one-sided. It exists specifically to meet the needs of the client. It is not reciprocal in the same way personal relationships are. This also sets therapists apart from practitioners of other modalities (Western medicine and holistic), who usually don't have to uphold such strict boundaries in the area of personal relationships with patients or clients. I share more about this in the next section.

The Difference Between Mental Health Therapists and Other Health Practitioners

Unlike practitioners who offer physical modalities (acupuncturists, chiropractors, and massage therapists), therapists adopt a specific *way of being* that affects how they relate to the client. This includes the personal information they choose to share, the types of jokes they tell, and perhaps even the entertainment they discuss.

This isn't to say practitioners of physical modalities don't practice boundaries and professionalism, but it's not the same.

Therapists offer a relationship as the primary modality. With other practitioners, the physical modality comes first, and the relationship is secondary. Because of this, there is more room for other practitioners to share about their families and personal lives because they can do so while still providing the service the client is paying for, whereas therapists have a smaller permission field for sharing personal matters because it can interfere with the service being offered. Not only does it take up valuable time that the client is paying for, but it could also impact the therapist–client relationship.

An example is a chiropractor who shares a love of college sports with a patient. They may enjoy discussing games or swapping tailgating stories. This can all be done during an appointment, in between the patient sharing about any pain or symptoms they're experiencing and the chiropractor performing adjustments. A chiropractor does not have to adopt a persona or different way of being with patients to do their job. As far as sports updates go, it's not that therapists *can't* discuss these things with clients. It's just that it may detract from the service the clients are paying for.

An Important Distinction Between Western Medical Providers (Including Therapists) and Holistic Practitioners

It's important to be aware of the power differential that is present with Western medical providers and their patients. For the purposes of this chapter, I'm referring to physicians, nurse practitioners, PA-C, physical therapists, psychiatrists, psychologists, and mental health therapists when I use the term *Western medical practitioners*. Even though chiropractors have a medical license, I consider them holistic practitioners because they do not diagnose or prescribe medication.

There is a power differential between *every* type of practitioner and their clients or patients. However the power differential is greater with Western medical and mental health practitioners because they are given more power and authority than practitioners outside the medical system. This is evidenced by how their influence extends to the other systems (legal, military, and academic).

What Western medical providers—particularly mental health therapists—think, say, and document matters to the other major systems and impacts people's lives in a way that feedback from other health and wellness practitioners does not.

For example, in the military, when a soldier's ability to perform their job is called into question, they're required to submit documentation from a licensed medical or mental health provider. The specific documentation requirements vary depending on the condition being evaluated, and whether it involves physical health, mental health, or both. While the soldier can technically submit any documentation they choose, the required documents are those from Western medical providers (physicians, nurse practitioners, PA-C, physical therapists, psychiatrists, psychologists, and mental health therapists). Documentation from licensed providers within the medical system carry the most weight and are used to determine whether soldiers are mentally and physically fit to perform their military job, deploy, and in some cases, continue their military career. The same is true with the legal system. Documentation from an acupuncturist or chiropractor simply does not hold the same weight in court proceedings, even though they have also undergone extensive training, completed supervised clinical hours, passed multiple exams, and met the requirements for continuing education credits.

As I was writing this book, there was one question that surfaced repeatedly on the subject of authority in the medical system:

Why is authority needed if the goal is just to help people?

The closer I look, the more I see the overlap between the medical and legal systems. I will share more about mental health providers acting in punitive or disciplinary ways in Chapter 16.

Therapists' Reputation in the Community

Another way the mental health therapist role is different from other practitioners is it's usually intertwined with other personality programs, most of which use the currency of virtue to earn approval. Therapists are seen as the guardian angels of society and are expected to be examples of kindness and compassion. Their views on certain topics may carry more weight than the typical person's, and they're used as a measurement of what is right, good, noble, and true. Speaking of public perception, people think nothing of asking therapists for a reduced rate when they would never even consider asking a PA-C, nurse practitioner, or MD for the same.

My point is that there's a lot tied up in the therapist job position that is important to acknowledge.

Chapter 8

How the Therapist Role Can Function as a Mask

The Internal Family Systems (IFS) model was created by Richard Schwartz and is a framework for conceptualizing our internal world. The word *family* is used in IFS to mean our internal family. This includes all the different aspects of our personality and the parts of ourselves that we accentuate, as well as the parts of ourselves that we may hide or downplay.

IFS is different from EMDR or Brainspotting in that it is a way of viewing our human condition, instead of a therapeutic modality used to directly target traumatic memories. The IFS model can help us work with the parts of ourselves that were affected by past events and can be used alongside EMDR or Brainspotting, but they have different purposes.

IFS is based on the idea that we all have a true self, but over the course of our lives, we create different protector parts—or personas—to ensure we stay safe and get our needs met. You can think of a protector part as a mask. Parts exhibit different types of behaviors, and when explored, they often have an age and a specific memory attached to them.

An example is a young girl who is punished for having below-average grades on her report card in third grade. As a result, she develops perfectionistic tendencies and becomes an overachiever to protect herself from punishment, criticism, and shame (external and internal consequences). She eventually becomes a college professor and enters an environment where perfectionism and overachieving are rewarded, and perhaps even required at times. When we view this woman through the IFS lens, we can see how perfectionism and overachievement are the protector parts that were created from the trauma of being punished for her grades as a child. The woman has an inner-child aspect that is trying to stay safe and possibly earn validation and approval through her role as a professor. In this way, her choice of vocation is heavily impacted by her unresolved childhood wounding.

While having protector parts is extremely common and not intrinsically negative, they usually outlive their usefulness and become maladaptive at some point. For example, the woman's "professor" part can become problematic if she decides she's no longer willing or able to continue overachieving or pursuing perfection. That's why building a life around our wounds may work for a time but is usually not sustainable long term.

People wear all kinds of masks to be accepted, feel important, and access a sense of safety in the world. However, because protector parts were formed out of fear and with survival in mind, their methods can be unsophisticated and immature. They can even get us into trouble if we don't have self-awareness, or if the part is emotionally or physically reactive. Protector parts take their jobs very seriously, so by the time we reach adulthood, their behaviors can be extreme and pretty deeply ingrained. The more awareness we can cultivate around our different protector parts—including behaviors they exhibit, what triggers them to step forward, and what they're protecting us from—the higher the likelihood that we'll be able to unblend from our protector parts and ensure they aren't running the show. Our adult self needs to be in the driver's seat.

For many therapists, the therapist role is a protector part, or a mask. It may have been formed at a young age as a result of being expected to provide emotional support to a parent. Understanding this is important to get the most out of the book, so I'll say it again in a different way: it is not unusual for the therapist role to be a mask that functions to protect the therapist's true self. While we shouldn't be ashamed of having protector parts that occasionally step in on our behalf, it is important to realize when we are leading with a protector part (mask self), or interfacing with someone else's.

We *all* have protector parts, not just therapists.

However, the "therapist" part has the potential to cause more harm because of the service they're offering and the authority they're given.

See below for ways the therapist role can function as a protector part (mask self) and serve a purpose beyond monetary gain or altruism.

- **Providing access to personal power through affiliation with the system**

  As long as the Western mental health system occupies a position of authority in society and is acknowledged as the predominant paradigm, working within it can serve as a status symbol. It may also boost the ego's need to be considered important, prestigious, and acclaimed (even vicariously).

- **Trying to fix or rescue others to feel needed and avoid abandonment**

  Rescuing others can be chemically and hormonally addicting in that it often provides both a dopamine hit and an adrenaline rush. This is especially true for those who adopted rescuer tendencies at a young age as a means of earning love and approval.

- **Using the role to avoid their own healing work**

  Overfocusing on others allows us to avoid ourselves. At a minimum, it serves as a distraction. In many cases, there's also a need to secure external validation or be viewed in a favorable way (competent, knowledgeable, prudent, principled, morally upstanding, and even superior). Receiving validation from others can go a long way in making up for what we lack internally, at least in the short term.

- **Diagnosing people in their personal lives to protect against the pain of rejection**

  I see this a lot on social media, particularly pertaining to romantic relationships. I believe the idea behind it is that it hurts less if we deem the person who rejected us as unwell in some way. Because therapists are authorized to use the DSM-5 to assign diagnostic labels, their opinion of people's mental health carries more weight, even outside the clinical setting.

- **Using others' problems to feel better about their own life**

  Therapists may compare themselves to clients to prove to themselves they're doing okay and to avoid their own healing work.

If you are considering whether to work with a mental health therapist, it may be a good time to decide whether you're comfortable working with someone who is potentially wearing a mask in place of their true self when addressing your mental and emotional concerns.

While writing this section, I explored whether it's possible for therapists to show up as their true selves within the current mental health system. I concluded that it is not. This is because they are given a list of rules to follow and guidelines to adhere to.

The way I see it, you're either following a predetermined set of rules *or* you're embodying your true self, being fully present in the moment, and using your internal guidance to navigate the situation.

You can't do both.

Questions pertaining to the true self vs. the masked self:

- If I'm being brave and showing up as my true self in a vulnerable moment, is it okay with me that the other person may not be?
- Is it even possible to fully embody my true self in the presence of someone else's masked self?
- How does the presence of a power differential impact my ability to access my true self?

For those interested in learning more about Internal Family Systems, I highly recommend visiting the IFS Institute website provided in the Resources section at the end of this book. It offers a more in-depth explanation of the IFS model, as well as book recommendations, videos, and online trainings.

Chapter 9
Safety in Clinical Settings

Now that we've covered a little on the therapist role and the secondary benefits it can offer, I'm sharing more about safety in clinical settings. For the purposes of this chapter, I'm using the word *safety* primarily to mean mental and emotional safety. However, I also discuss the potential loss of agency and autonomy, which can quickly become a matter of physical safety as well.

I want to start by challenging the following ideas:

- Therapists are non-negotiably safe people.
- There are no risks associated with entering the clinical setting.

You may view therapy as an opportunity to sit on a couch with a nice-looking person wearing a cardigan who will smile, nod, and agree with everything you say while you share stories about your whole life in great detail. Your plan may be to schedule a therapy session, tell the therapist what's on your mind, see what they say, and go from there. You may assume you'll be informed of all the options and will maintain your agency and autonomy throughout the entire process.

However, this is not always the case.

Unfortunately, there is a risk with crossing the threshold and entering the therapist's office. By showing up in that space, you're giving them the power to document something that could affect you in a custody battle or affect your eligibility for certain job positions. I would say the chances of this happening increase exponentially the more "severe" you present, as the therapist may view you as a liability.

**If we're not able to show up fully without the possibility of
having our personal freedoms revoked, is it actually safe?**

This question is deeply personal, and I do not pretend to have the answer. It depends on what you're seeking and whether it's worth the risk. As with most things in life, there is a trade-off.

There is also what I see as the million-dollar question, which, try as I might, I couldn't find a great place for in this manuscript, but strongly felt it needed to be included somewhere:

Who Are These People Anyway?

Therapists are taught to use minimal self-disclosure; therefore, clients don't really know who they're talking to. The therapist's life could be a train wreck, and the client would never know. They may use their work as a therapist to escape all their problems and be very skilled at compartmentalizing. As I sit here today, I can confidently say that some of the most challenging personalities I've ever encountered worked within the medical or mental health system. Unfortunately, it is not uncommon for clinicians to talk about their clients in judgmental, condescending, and dehumanizing ways, diagnose everyone in their personal lives, or have some type of addiction. They may also have poor boundaries, lack consideration for others in the office, and overshare about personal health matters, family drama, or dating. I don't doubt this occurs in other professions as well, but when you consider it within the context of what therapists claim to help with and the power we give them, it's a little concerning.

Speaking of encountering challenging personalities in the mental health field, I'm reminded of the time I joined a group private practice following the completion of my full-time military position. In joining the practice, I was provided with office space, client referrals, and the office manager's help with scheduling appointments, taking payments, and billing insurance companies. In return, the practice received a percentage of each therapy session. This freed me up to spend the majority of my time and energy on clients. Overall, I'd say it was a pretty good gig . . . until it wasn't.

While I can look back now and see the warning signs, at the time, I tried to just focus on working with clients and further developing my clinical skills. I had an entire caseload of clients who were a great fit, and it was awesome to see them steadily make progress toward their goals. I'm actually getting a little sad as I write this, because it was so perfect for a time, but I unfortunately know how the story ends. This is where I would insert a sad face emoji if I were writing a blog entry, but I'm not sure that's allowed in books.

Anyway, at some point things took a turn, and the office environment no longer felt supportive. There was constant conflict, and it felt very tense. While I tried to act as a buffer between the staff and my clients, I'm sure the clients became aware of the dysfunction despite my best efforts. Around this time, I attended a conference in Chicago and was so excited to implement everything I learned. However, when I got back to the office, I found that things were even worse than when I'd left. I believe the issue of the week was who was allowed to use the "big office." Considering I saw most clients after hours and was often the only one there, I found this issue to be complete nonsense and could not even pretend to engage with it.

Because I saw no end in sight and knew the key players were not interested in unity and cohesion, I felt it was time to leave the group practice and start my own. This ended up being the catalyst for moving out of state! I informed the owner of the practice (who was also a therapist) that I was moving but would allow plenty of time to inform clients and transition out properly. We had a conversation that I thought resulted in us being on the same page and agreeing on a plan for my departure. I continued business as usual for another week or so before having the idea of offering telehealth for the clients who wanted to continue working with me after I moved. I came up with this idea with continuity of care in mind, and I still think it was the most ethical option for easing the transition and preventing interruptions in the hard work the clients were in the middle of. Since I was never asked to sign a non-compete agreement, I didn't expect it to be a problem. I actually thought the owner of the practice would be supportive, but unfortunately, that was not the case.

We could've easily worked out an arrangement that would have kept me in the practice on paper for a few months so I could see those clients remotely, but that idea was never entertained. Instead, the owner emailed my entire caseload between one and five a.m. one Friday morning, informing them of my departure before I had a chance to tell them myself. She not only said I was leaving but also that it was happening a lot sooner than we'd agreed upon. It made it look like I was either choosing to leave abruptly or being made to (perhaps for disciplinary reasons) and that I planned to do so without telling them. This was not only extremely unprofessional but also unethical. Group practice owners rarely have a reason to directly contact therapists' clients, other than in cases of sickness or literal death. Doing so creates confusion and can negatively impact the therapist-client relationship due to undermining the therapist.

Over the course of the next week, I learned even more about what information was disseminated via those early-morning emails, including when my last day would be! This put me in the very difficult position of having to explain to clients that I was, in fact, leaving, but that I did not intend for my departure to be handled this way. I was careful not to say anything that would reflect unfavorably on the practice or the owner in case clients wanted to continue with them.

As far as my day-to-day work and my efforts to ethically and properly transition out, I was informed in an email that the practice owner had appointed her husband as the director of operations and that he would be my point of contact from then on. I'm not sure if I ever saw the owner again—other than passing her in the hallway once in between sessions.

I will never forget trying to log into our electronic medical record to input my visit notes (required documentation for every session) and getting an "Access denied" message. This made it impossible for me to update charts until I created my own form to document clients' progress. Following my last session with each client, I gave the hard copy notes to the office manager to be uploaded into the system. This not only ensured that I stayed in compliance with guidelines pertaining to clinical records, it would also assist the next therapist in picking up where we'd left off if the client stayed with the practice. My goal was a seamless transition for all, which was completely unrealistic considering the circumstances—but man, how I love that younger version of myself who tried so hard anyway.

I share this story for several reasons. It illustrates just how much can go on behind the scenes of a single therapy session and how the ethics and professionalism of the practice—or lack thereof—can impact both therapists and clients (directly or indirectly). It's also a reminder that just because someone is in a leadership position or has been in the field for a long time, it doesn't mean they're willing or able to navigate transitions skillfully, or that they have the clients' best interest in mind. When there is administrative breakdown or discord among team members, the clients often get caught in the crossfire.

At this point, I have no hard feelings toward the practice owner and I'm grateful for the learning experiences she facilitated in every aspect. While I feel my departure could've been handled better, I understand that no one is immune to being triggered and reacting defensively, myself included. The entire situation activated my own survival responses in a way that was similar to aspects of my military career, so I used it as an opportunity to notice a pattern and take ownership of the parts of myself that seemed to attract these situations.

Questions to consider while working with a practitioner:

- Is this person someone I need to be consulting regarding life management?
- Do I have enough information to determine this?
- Do I trust them enough to judge me in the areas of personality, morals, functioning, worldview, and basically the totality of the inner workings of my mind?
- Should anyone have that power over another person?

Chapter 10

Therapists Are Human Too

If you find yourself feeling bad for the therapists I mention in my examples, you are not alone. I can certainly access compassion for them, and for the less experienced version of myself who inevitably made mistakes and may have unintentionally perpetuated some of the things I've now chosen to write about. No one is perfect or infallible, and we can only operate from the level of consciousness that we're at.

If therapists are also human, have blind spots, and are just as likely to project or operate out of their own wounding as anyone else, then maybe we should take that into account when choosing how much emphasis to put on what they say and document. Perhaps what is conveyed in their notes should take up a little less space on the pie chart. It may also be a good idea to hold the labels they use with a looser grip.

At the present time, I would not say the system reflects therapists' humanity or allows for their inevitable shortcomings.

They are granted authority as if they are superhuman and viewed as the experts, to the point that a single piece of paper containing their opinion, signature, and time and date stamp can change the entire trajectory of someone's life.

I'm focusing on practitioners in the mental health system because that is my background and experience. However, this section also applies to individuals occupying leadership positions within the other major systems, including the military, politics, and churches. Basically, anyone who is overseeing lives—physical, spiritual, mental, or emotional lives.

Chapter 11
Dynamics That Can Occur in Clinical Settings

The following are dynamics or scenarios you may encounter in the clinical mental health setting. While they can be observed in other facets of society, they have the potential to cause the most harm in environments where there is a power differential.

#1 Parentification and the Rescuer, Victim, Perpetrator Triangle

To parentify someone is to place them in the role of a parent. This can happen anytime we look to another person to fulfill our emotional needs or tell us what to do, think, or feel. When we parentify someone, we place them on a pedestal. Because we view ourselves as inferior to them, we may feel disempowered or experience an age regression during interactions. Parentification can occur with people, ideologies, and even entire systems.

Parentification is a form of codependency and is especially common in those who have attachment wounds from childhood. While it's normal to occasionally find ourselves in codependent relationships due to convenience or mutual need, it's important to periodically assess if what we are seeking is actually available through that avenue. If it's not, we may be setting ourselves up for disappointment.

All too often, people look to someone they deem an authority figure to play a parental role in their lives, then they end up feeling confused and betrayed when the person they've parentified inevitably lets them down. It's also not unusual to choose a person or an organization to recreate dysfunctional childhood dynamics and to relate to them the same way we did an *abusive* parent. This can result in a trauma bond, which I share more about in the next section.

As a general rule, casting someone in the role of a parent or playing the role of another adult's parent usually indicates we've entered into what's called the Drama Triangle and are playing one or more of the following roles:

- Rescuer
- Victim
- Perpetrator[4]

Usually, if we're playing one of these roles, we're playing all of them, but in different areas of our life. Think about it. Someone who has a stressful job and feels like a victim at work may abuse and neglect their children at home; or a person with unresolved childhood trauma may spend their whole life trying to rescue people from what they went through.

The rescuer-victim-perpetrator dynamic can show up in the mental health therapy setting if the therapist acts to rescue the client from difficult emotions or life situations (by giving advice, etc.). Attempting to rescue others can cause us to unintentionally override people's boundaries, and it ultimately reinforces their victimhood. Rescuing people from their hardships—and potentially the consequences of their own actions—temporarily makes the rescuer feel good, but it's rarely sustainable over the long term. It's also not unusual for rescuers to default to martyr or victim mode when they get tired or burned out. This is usually because they feel overwhelmed by everyone relying on them. However, this happens because, over time, they created a dependency on themselves by rescuing people.

When we're embodying either the rescuer or the victim role, we can become so overidentified with the prey animal that we don't realize we have the ability to be the predator. I was introduced to this idea through a book by Kimberly Ann Johnson called *Call of the Wild: How We Heal Trauma, Awaken Our Power, and Use It for Good.*[5]

---

4. Stephen B. Karpman, *A Game Free Life*, 1ˢᵗ ed. (Drama Triangle Publications, 2014) 24–26.

5. Kimberly Ann Johnson, *Call of the Wild: How We Heal Trauma, Awaken Our Own Power, and Use It For Good* (New York, NY: Harperwave, 2021) 107.

This relates to what I mentioned earlier about trying so hard to help someone that we overstep and end up causing harm.

A few reasons we can default to rescue mode are:

- We're uncomfortable with others' discomfort.
- We want to feel needed or important.
- We want to gain a sense of control.

Healing my own rescuer tendencies turned out to be the beginning of the end for my therapist career. I realized that I'd spent so much of my life attuning to everyone *except myself* that I barely knew who I was apart from that. Over time, I'd developed the ability to basically merge with others—or act as a chameleon—and morph into whatever they needed me to be. This is called self-abandonment, and it is common among people who choose helping others as a career.

By the time I became a therapist, I'd already been self-abandoning for years. My top two personality programs were the perfectionist and the performer. They originated in childhood where there was a very large emphasis placed on outward appearance, social approval, and virtue. I earned approval by showing what a good person I was and how much I could help others. My thoughts, feelings, and opinions came secondary to those around me to the point that I lost the ability to discern what they were.

I realized while writing this book that I denied my own humanity long before the system got a chance to.

Once self-abandonment becomes a way of life and a matter of survival, we become a match for jobs and relationships that reinforce it.

Simply put, we write ourselves out of the story before anyone else can.

My story is unique, as is everyone's, but it is not rare. We all do this stuff, and if left unexamined, we'll continue to. It works until it doesn't!

I reached a crossroads in early 2023 when I realized that I could either attune to the person sitting in front of me (who was often in emotional distress) *or* I could speak my truth; but I could rarely do both. At the time, the idea that I may not actually want to meet every person where they are, or that I can't necessarily promise to be a safe place for everyone all the time was a little destabilizing. After all, who am I if not a source of strength and comfort for others? What does this say about me?

While I could've taken that opportunity to beat myself over the head with shame and judgment, the only thing my decision actually said about me was that I was ready to have a different experience.

It's such a basic and neutral story. I'll take it!

Questions for exploring rescuer tendencies:

- What if I never help anyone again? Am I still worthy of love and belonging?
- What am I avoiding by rescuing others from their pain?
- Why am I so quick to enter into other people's worlds and vacate my own?
- What benefit am I getting from my role as a helper/fixer, and is there a healthier way to meet that need?

#2 Trauma Bonds

Anytime parentification or a rescuer-victim dynamic is present, there's also a high likelihood a trauma bond has formed. One definition of a trauma bond is when we become overly attached to something that is harming us. Think of holding on to a rope that you think is saving your life, but it's also giving you rope burn and making your hands bleed. I will discuss in the next few paragraphs how trauma bonds are functional and, therefore, meet a need—at least temporarily. This is why they may not appear harmful in the beginning; however, they can really take a toll long-term.

Trauma bonds can be extremely complex due to their symbiotic nature. I use the term *symbiotic* because both parties benefit from the arrangement on some level. While at first glance, it may appear that only the "victim" is benefiting, the "rescuer" is usually benefiting as well. As I mentioned in Chapter 8, the rescuer's efforts to help may seem 100 percent altruistic, but the more likely scenario is that they need to be needed. This is why the bond is parasitic in nature—both people are extracting something from the other in ways that can become very draining and even abusive over time.

Trauma bonds do not only occur between people. They can occur with substances, jobs, foods, and entire organizations or systems.

When trauma bonds occur between people, both parties are required to abandon their true selves in order to play out the rescuer and victim roles. This type of relationship is not conducive to growth and evolution. Instead, it enables both people to continue their current behavior patterns. Usually, if one person heals, the relationship is toast—at least in its current form. That's not to say the relationship can't shift to accommodate healing and growth, but both parties have to be willing to engage differently and thus forgo the benefits of the rescuer and victim roles.

When the following emotions and behaviors originate from the same place, there's a high likelihood that a trauma bond is present:

- Love and pain
- Acceptance and rejection
- Praise and devaluation
- Information and withholding of information

While the formation of trauma bonds isn't usually intentional, they can still be really damaging. It can also be extremely challenging to extricate oneself from them due to their addictive nature. The addiction is to our own stress hormones, as opposed to the person or relationship. The intermittent and unpredictable reinforcement inherent in trauma bonds results in chronically elevated stress hormones (adrenaline and cortisol), and overusing dopamine pathways due to being inconsistently rewarded with attention, validation, and connection—which results in us constantly seeking more.

Sidenote: A trauma bond is a symptom of a deeper issue. Similar to an addiction to alcohol or other substances, trauma bonds with people serve to protect or distract us from underlying wounds.

When viewed in this way, it becomes apparent that even if we ended every relationship that has characteristics of a trauma bond, we would still be left with the root cause that led to participating in them to begin with.

The formation of a trauma bond often indicates a lack of self-trust, or a belief in our own helplessness, incompetence, or brokenness. Once these underlying wounds are healed, trauma bonds will usually balance out naturally or end altogether, since there's no longer a need for them.

While I used to be annoyed by the idea that all of our relationships mirror the relationship we have with ourselves, I've seen over the years how it is true in most cases. This is why we can learn so much by exploring our relationships with people, jobs, living situations, and even organizations and systems.

Unfortunately, it's not unusual for clients to become trauma bonded to their mental health therapist due to the power differential and the one-sided nature of the relationship. Because clients usually know very little about their therapist, it's easy to project positive traits and attributes onto them, whether or not the therapist actually exhibits those positive qualities. It is also not unusual for clients to view their therapist as superior and to fall into the habit of looking to the therapist for direction in place of their own internal guidance.

While trauma bonds can occur with any type of practitioner—or between any two people—the ones that develop between clients and mental health therapists tend to be more complex and energetically charged due to the reasons I mentioned above.

Another reason the therapist–client relationship is conducive to trauma bonds is the frequent discussion of emotionally charged material. When a client tells their therapist about a traumatic event, it is not unusual for their nervous system to become activated as if they're reliving it. This is because their body believes the event is happening in the present. A sign this is happening is the client exhibits shallow breathing, sweaty palms, and redness or flushing, indicating their stress hormones are elevated. When therapists and clients regularly enter into these heightened states with one another, it creates a feeling of "we're in this together," as if an alliance is being formed. This can occur consciously or unconsciously and add a layer of complexity to the relationship.

Trauma bonds between therapists and clients may result in the client becoming dependent on the therapist and feeling incapable of making decisions or managing their life without them. A client may also feel as if they require their therapist to tell them when they're healed and can discontinue therapy. However, because of the trauma bond, the client may not present as stable enough to discontinue therapy, so the therapist may actually believe they need to continue. This is a double bind that can be challenging for both parties to navigate.

By this point, you may be asking yourself if it matters whether you tend to parentify people, or if you're participating in a few trauma bonds here and there.

After all, what's the big deal?

Trauma bonds keep us stuck in an arrested developmental state where we have very little access to our adult self. They stunt our growth and development and keep us dependent and disempowered. Unfortunately, our disempowerment rarely stays contained within the context of the relationship, but instead it ripples out and infiltrates other aspects of our lives. Once we buy into the belief that we're incomplete on our own, we live as if it is true then start to see it mirrored back to us in the external world. This is the primary way we create our own reality.

To bring it full circle, when we're in a trauma bond, we can start to overidentify with the way we're being viewed—or see ourselves through the other person's eyes—then take it as the truth of who we are. If they need us to be sick, weak, and disempowered, we will feel sick, weak, and disempowered. It's like we're showing up in their movie and playing a role we've been cast in, even if it's a very hard role to play and is ultimately to our detriment. I've personally experienced this with relationships in the past due to operating on the belief that I needed the person to stay in my life. I've since realized that any relationship that requires me to sacrifice my well-being in order to maintain it is not worth the trade-off.

As with any relational dynamic, the components of a trauma bond are on a continuum and have a tendency to fluctuate; therefore, it's important to stay flexible in your assessment of the situation instead of becoming too concerned with the exact criteria. What matters more than anything is how you feel in the relationship. If it feels addicting or all-consuming, you may want to get curious about that. You could try taking some time and space to explore what comes up for you in the absence of the other party. You could also try setting boundaries around the relationship in the areas of your time, accessibility, and emotional investment. Healthy people appreciate clear expectations and guidelines, so you may find that implementing a few boundaries results in more respectful, productive, and fulfilling interactions going forward.

When it comes to preventing trauma bonds with medical practitioners (even holistic ones), doing your own research, not placing them on a pedestal, and getting a second—or even third—opinion when deciding whom to work with can go a long way.

#3 "Break You Down and Build You Back Up" . . . on the Therapist's Terms

"Break you down and build you back up" is a military phrase used primarily in the basic training environment. Basic training is the initial training soldiers enter after they complete their recruitment paperwork and are accepted into the military. It is broken down into three distinct phases, with the goal of humbling soldiers on the front end to ensure they're teachable, then putting them through a variety of training activities so they can exhibit mastery of their soldier skills. While this makes sense in a military environment where soldiers are being prepared for a literal war, the people who show up in the mental health system have already been through their own personal war but can unfortunately walk right back into the same dynamics.

We see this in the therapeutic setting when someone schedules a session with a therapist to explore a few minor life stressors, then are told they're deeply troubled and will require regular therapy and medication for the foreseeable future. They may start to believe they're inherently defective and feel dependent on the therapist or system to fix them. The concern is not necessarily that the therapist is providing feedback. It's that they're doing so through a deficit-based lens with a vested interest in the client needing them.

On some level, we're all healing from being interpreted through the lens of other people's wounds and limiting beliefs. Most of the things we don't like about ourselves are probably projections from a less conscious—if not entirely narcissistic—perspective. Think about it. Our self-concept is formed when we are young children. During that time, our primary source of feedback is our parents and immediate family. This means we were told who we were by twenty-year-olds, and we had no choice but to believe them. However, many people still subscribe to those beliefs!

Yes, I'm referring to our parents' perspectives as a narcissistic projection without knowing if they actually exhibited traits associated with narcissism because of the emotional maturity level they were most likely operating from. Even if they tried hard and meant well, they were probably still overwhelmed and lacked the capacity to connect and attune to us in all the ways we needed.

To bring us full circle to the present day, the lens through which we're viewed matters. If we're going to choose someone to listen and act as a sounding board for us during some of our most vulnerable moments, it's important to choose someone who doesn't have a dog in the fight *and* is operating from a place of wholeness within themselves. Therapists' ideas surrounding mental health—and the human experience in general—greatly impact the feedback clients receive in a therapy session.

Practitioners are only capable of taking us as far as they've gone themselves, and they can only meet us as deeply as they've met themselves.

Even if therapists want nothing more than for clients to be magically healed and to never come back again, they're still evaluating them through a deficit-based lens. When I use the term *deficit-based lens*, I'm referring to the mental health system's focus on what's wrong with a person, as opposed to what's right about them (their gifts and strengths). Similar to editors, therapists are paid to identify errors and weaknesses. The fact that therapists often focus on what's wrong isn't intrinsically negative, but if you're looking for their approval and hoping to come away from your therapy session with a gold star or A+, you may want to adjust your expectations.

I have experienced firsthand how helpful it can be to bounce ideas off someone when I'm feeling stuck or lost. I have also benefited from hearing other perspectives, especially when I'm too close to the situation, or when I'm unable to access neutrality for any reason. However, when it comes to giving someone access to my inner world, I've developed some strict guidelines over the years to help me identify safe people. This started by first realizing that I have an inner world that not everyone deserves access to; only then could I fully step into my role as gatekeeper of it!

My criteria for safe people:

- They don't benefit from me staying stuck, and have no interest in creating a dependency on themselves.
- They're healthy enough not to project onto me. They can see me clearly.
- They can partner with me in the belief that I am whole regardless of the outcome of the current situation.

Once again, these are just some things to be aware of when deciding how much value to place on therapists' feedback—or whether to even pursue it.

Chapter 12
Additional Considerations When Navigating Clinical Settings

The Tendency for Therapists to Overdiagnose

I am using the term *overdiagnose* to mean assigning a diagnostic label when the client does not meet the diagnostic criteria. I would also define overdiagnosing as assigning a diagnostic label if the client's symptoms only surface during periods of transition or heightened stress before returning to baseline.

This is hard to describe since the diagnostic criteria are subjective to begin with, and there's naturally a lot of variability when it comes to human behavior in general. That being said, I'll share two reasons it can occur and give examples of what I consider to be overdiagnosing.

1. The therapist's clinical experience (or lack thereof)

Therapists with a narrow range of clinical experience may be overly reactive to symptoms and quick to label them. This can happen if they have only worked with one or two populations during their career, such as special-needs children, refugees, or veterans. Therapists may also be more reactive to symptoms if they've specialized in an extremely specific treatment area, such as addiction recovery, eating disorders, or in a hospital rehab unit. If this is the case, they may not have exposure to a wide range of presentations and may be operating within a narrow scope. Therapists can also be overly reactive to symptoms and quick to diagnose when they're transitioning from working with the general public to working with a specific population.

I saw this firsthand in the military when the National Guard hired civilian contractors to conduct mental health assessments during the soldiers' yearly physicals and pre-deployment screenings. This was normally the behavioral health officers' responsibility, but we had a small team at the time and, as I mentioned earlier, over nine thousand soldiers. We needed to divide and conquer!

It was all fun and games until we logged into the computer system on Monday morning to review reports from the weekend and saw that approximately 70 percent of the soldiers had been flagged for either a mental or physical health concern. After using our Nancy Drew skills to figure out what on earth happened, we realized the civilian clinicians were marking soldiers non-deployable or recommending they not be issued a military weapon if they checked some combination of the following boxes: "experiences anger," "owns a firearm," and "consumes alcohol." While I understand the concerns with someone being unable to manage their anger, *mishandling* a weapon, and drinking *to excess*, just because a soldier checks a few boxes on an online questionnaire does not mean they're irresponsible or unsafe. Also, we're talking about the Army National Guard in the southern part of the US here, so if we're looking for people who never check any of those boxes, we may be out of luck!

The point is, it's important to know your population. There are so many cultural (and subcultural) factors that come into play, and without placing the person and what they're sharing within the proper context, the results will be skewed, or we'll miss the intent entirely. This was called "person in environment" in school, and it's a reminder that the big picture is important.

I actually don't blame the civilian contractors for flagging such a high percentage of the service members. I'm sure it was very distressing to be granted insight into the soldiers' inner world, and it probably did not feel accurate or ethical to indicate in a clinical note that they were okay when they seemed anything but okay. They could have also been experiencing a double bind that is ever-present with mental health practitioners working with the military population: Military leaders want to be told that their entire unit is physically *and* mentally fit for military service, including deployment. However, that is rarely—if ever—the case. The more likely scenario is that a percentage of the unit is unfit for a variety of reasons, which means the commander will need to find replacements if they're scheduled to deploy within the next few months. Because the military is composed of humans (not robots), service members frequently disclose medical concerns that require time and specialized interventions to heal properly. In case you're wondering, being the one to deliver this news to commanders is even less fun than it sounds!

Anyway, back to the civilian contractors. Ultimately, we decided that the most appropriate way to utilize their services was to have them conduct brief assessments with each soldier to obtain relevant information that the military clinical team would review, instead of asking the civilian clinicians to comment on soldiers' deployability or whether they should be issued a weapon. This seemed to be an improvement all around. It not only freed up the contractors to focus their attention on the areas they were most comfortable with, it also provided the military clinical team with the information we needed to determine which soldiers were good to go and which ones needed more time or support.

I shared this story to illustrate how clinicians' experiences affect the way they practice. If clinicians lack exposure to, or understanding of, the unique challenges of a certain population, that will be reflected in their clinical assessment. This may include assigning diagnostic labels that clinicians with more experience would not feel the need to use.

Once again, it is extremely important to consider the overall context and the person's environment when assessing or treating their mental health. My military experience tends to be the easiest to draw from when sharing stories and examples because it's such a distinct subculture, but the tendency for clinicians to overdiagnose or to be somewhat out of touch with the population they're working with can show up in all facets of mental health.

Sidenote: Speaking of double binds that exist for mental health professionals in the military, there is an idea that clinicians' licenses are safe—and maybe even untouchable—within that system. However, that wasn't necessarily the case. I cannot count the number of times the military put me in a position that resulted in me feeling extremely clinically unprotected.

During my time in the Army, I was frequently asked or told to do something that could have resulted in me losing my license. However, when I consulted with the social work licensing board on one particularly challenging situation, they had nothing to offer and actually deferred to the military. So much for a little guidance! They were basically saying, "You're on your own, but don't do the wrong thing." As tempting as it was to take the bait, I did not think for one minute that telling the licensing board, "The colonel made me do it," would've been enough to get me off the hook had I been investigated.

Situations like these motivated me to become more skilled at communicating my professional and clinical boundaries in the military, which came with a different set of challenges, but at least my license was safe.

2.   The Therapist's Lack of Self-Awareness

The second reason therapists may overdiagnose is having deficits or blind spots in their awareness of themselves. As a general rule, if a person lacks insight into their own behaviors, they will have very little context for others' behaviors and may label them as abnormal, or even disordered. In clinical settings, this could result in therapists being overly reactive to symptoms and assigning diagnostic labels quicker and more often than they would if they had more personal experience navigating symptoms, or just more insight into their own inner world. As I mentioned earlier, any job that encourages or requires people to overfocus on others can easily be used to avoid personal healing work.

A good example of something clinicians may not have experience with—and therefore may be reactive to—is dissociation. This is when we're physically present but mentally elsewhere, and to the extreme, it can cause problems. However, we all do it. No one is 100% present for the whole entire day, nor do we need to be. Some tasks allow us to zone out and take mental breaks, thank goodness! We also don't owe anyone an explanation of where our mind wanders, regardless of whether they feel entitled to it. Most people don't even realize they dissociate, so when they hear the term or see it written in a clinical record, it can be very alarming.

When I was practicing, if a client expressed concerns about dissociation, I made sure to provide education on it and help them explore their experiences and concerns. This was an attempt to normalize dissociation a little and hopefully neutralize some of the panic and shame it can evoke. My point is, if someone has never experienced dissociation—or doesn't realize they have—it's very easy to overreact to the idea of it.

Clients Feeling They Have Overshared

I remember sitting in a therapy session as the client in 2021 and feeling like the questions I was being asked during the initial assessment did not pertain to my treatment goals or reasons for scheduling the appointment. It seemed like the therapist was using leading questions in an attempt to guide me in a specific direction instead of just allowing me to share my concerns.

By that point in my life and career, I'd performed hundreds of intake assessments and knew that attempting to obtain information that is unrelated to the person's goals or just asking questions out of curiosity is unethical. Ironically, during my time in the military, I'd trained the other behavioral health officers on this exact thing. Since the goal was to determine whether the soldiers were mentally fit to deploy, we did not need to know every detail of their lives or gather an in-depth trauma history. The emphasis was on their current level of functioning and whether they could perform their military job. While the military does have a process in place for soldiers who need a more thorough psychological evaluation, trying to excavate deep, emotional material during a standard physical (either annual or pre-deployment) wouldn't have been appropriate for multiple reasons. This is an example of how important it is for therapists to be clear on their goals and intentions when performing assessments, then to stick to them!

Anyway, because I wasn't comfortable with this therapist or where I felt she was steering the session, I disengaged. I still believe this was a very healthy response to the situation. A less healthy response would have been thoroughly answering all her questions even though I was uncomfortable just because I felt I owed her this information.

Unfortunately, this happens all the time in clinical settings! The combination of the clinician feeling entitled to detailed personal information within the first few visits, and the inherent power differential present in all clinical settings can be a perfect storm. To answer questions we aren't comfortable with just because we don't know how to say no, or aren't aware we have a choice is a version of the freeze-and-fawn survival response (Appendix C).

Once again, I wish I could say this is rare in clinical settings, but it's not. People frequently share more than they're comfortable with, then leave with what's known as a vulnerability hangover. They may even feel manipulated on some level. However, because those who seek mental health treatment often have a history of surviving narcissistic abuse—including their perspective being invalidated or even denied altogether—they may doubt their own judgment and even gaslight themselves into thinking the therapist always knows best. The internal dialogue usually goes something like "After all, aren't I the 'crazy' one?"

On some level, this can feel like emotional rape, in that a personal boundary has been crossed. While I don't think it's usually intentional, it can be extremely confusing and retraumatizing to feel like you reached out for help and were taken advantage of in a moment of vulnerability. If you recognize yourself within this story, we've all been there! Whatever you said or did is okay. It was not your responsibility to know how to navigate this. In the presence of a power differential, it's easy to go into autopilot and defer to the professional. When we're caught off guard and our internal alarm bells are sounding, our bodies just default to what they know.

One last thing: The situation I described with the therapist was uncomfortable, and I feel she could have handled it better. However, I'm aware that within the mental health system, it is nearly impossible to avoid that dynamic entirely. That's the point here. Therapists are required to conduct a thorough assessment prior to formulating a treatment plan. It is filed in the client's medical record so the therapist can refer to it to measure treatment progress or produce it in case of an investigation or court proceeding. When conducting the assessment, it can be challenging to gauge the client's comfort level, especially when they aren't always sure themselves. Add to this the possibility that the client is in a freeze-or-fawn nervous system state and you have fertile ground for misunderstandings and boundary crossings.

The following phrase helped me remember this when navigating hierarchical structures both in the military and with therapy clients:

A "yes" isn't really a yes if someone doesn't have the freedom to use their "no"

. . .or if they don't realize they do.

Personal Share

While writing this section, I explored the ways I may have unintentionally encouraged clients to share more than they were comfortable with. I was operating on the belief that the more I knew, the more I could help them. I was also trying to be a good clinician, which meant I needed to conduct a thorough and in-depth assessment.

However, by the end of my time in both the military and the mental health system, I was experiencing guilt and discomfort during assessments because I couldn't guarantee that what the soldiers and therapy clients were sharing wouldn't be used against them in some way. The clients and soldiers felt comfortable with me and told me some very personal things, and may have felt betrayed when they were met with an unfavorable outcome. I don't blame them! I see now that I was playing the role of an abusive parent. Basically, I was saying, "I'm here for you. I've got your back," then some version of "Actually, no, I don't." or "Gotcha!" While I tried to communicate in a way that was both assertive and compassionate, it still felt like a bait and switch.

I couldn't have articulated this back then, but there was an exchange that went beyond money and time.

In both practice settings I was expected to use my interpersonal skills to put people at ease and build a rapport with them, only to turn around and assign a diagnostic label or say they were not fit for military service. It felt very inauthentic and like my best qualities were being used to meet the needs of the organization or system, as opposed to the person's. I was offering my personality and my full undivided attention in exchange for information. I was using who I was to accomplish a goal I did not consciously choose or consent to—or at least not one I fully understood. It felt like I was being both manipulated (by the organization) and manipulative (toward the clients and service members).

From my current vantage point, I can see that playing both sides is not only confusing for everyone involved, but it's also ineffective.

I'd also say the idea that I was pulling it off was somewhat of an illusion. In reality, the only reason that worked was because of the power differential. I got away with operating like that because the military and the mental health licensing board granted me authority.

The scenarios I described would never work in settings where the playing field was equal—nor should they! In order to do what was being asked of me in both military and civilian mental health practitioner roles, I was required to use passive-aggressive communication, vacillate between two contradictory roles, and somehow find a way to exist with mixed loyalties that were irreconcilable. I finally realized I couldn't cause a problem for someone, then immediately jump to the other side and attempt to fix it. Not only was it a total mind f*** for the other person, but it also resulted in me feeling like a sell-out.

While this is all very hard to sit with, I felt I needed to include it. These dynamics show up in every major system, especially mental health, medicine, law, and organized religion. Individuals working in these systems portray that they are there to help and that they can be trusted, but when people actually go to them, they flip the script or bring the hammer down. It turns out many of the people working in the systems aren't there for us after all. Their loyalty is to the system. It is not unusual for the information we share to be used against us. This is how engaging with the major systems can result in us being weaponized against ourselves, and even participating in our own captivity.

I also feel safe in saying that most people working within the systems— especially mental health and organized religion—are not actually equipped to handle the information they collect from people. In the rare instances where the individual is equipped, the system is not set up to provide the support needed. There's often no real help available, and in many cases, people actually end up feeling worse than before.

"The Doctor Knows Best"

One glaring problem with the "doctor knows best" mentality is that it's based on the assumption that the practitioner can actually understand what is going on with the client or patient. This requires them to be fully present with the person long enough to gain insight into what the person is experiencing. Depending on the clinical setting, this may not be possible. While therapists in a private practice setting usually spend fifty minutes with clients, mental health practitioners in emergency rooms, hospitals, and inpatient and outpatient clinics typically have very high caseloads and are afforded very little time with each patient.

In my experience, when it comes to inpatient psychiatric facilities, hospitals, and clinics, it is not unusual for intake assessments to be performed by a person who has a degree in the behavioral sciences, but who is not licensed to diagnose or treat mental health concerns. They may even be a graduate school intern. Oftentimes, the "intake person" will make a "diagnostic recommendation," then the doctor will sign off on it later. This splits the diagnostic process into two roles and increases the chances of inaccuracy. This is an example of how the diagnostic label is largely determined by the person you end up sitting across from and why it's important to hold labels with a loose hand.

I'm intentionally using broad language when explaining the intake process for psychiatric facilities because every facility operates differently. Regardless of attempts at standardization across the US, the reality is that every medical establishment has its own unique ways of staying in compliance, at least on paper. This may or may not translate to actual services rendered or guarantee the quality or effectiveness of those services. This also serves as a reminder that medical settings and their internal policies and procedures are not spotless or infallible. So, once again, it's just good to be aware of these things when determining how much emphasis to place on feedback from mental health practitioners.

Even if the clinician spends a lot of time with the patient, and gathers sufficient information about their concerns, the Western mental health model is so limited that there's still no guarantee the clinician will have a framework for what the client is experiencing. When I say the model is limited, I'm not only referring to the education and training mental health practitioners receive but also to the options they have to choose from when making clinical determinations and assigning diagnostic labels. Because of these limitations, even the most highly trained and credentialed practitioner in the mental health system may only be able to decipher a small percentage of what is going on with a person at any given time.

This is not a comment on the practitioner's competency. Instead, it's a reminder of how multifaceted we are as humans and how complex the interplay is between our mind, body, and spirit. While some mental health professionals are dedicated to getting to know their clients and patients and go out of their way to understand multiple aspects of the human condition to be more effective in their role, this is not always the case. Therefore, to automatically assume the doctor knows best is to set ourselves up for disappointment and perhaps even immeasurable harm.

The healthiest and most effective clinicians I've worked alongside are very quick to tell you that the patient or client knows themselves best. That awareness alone can make all the difference. Humility can take us far!

Chapter 13
Limitations of the Mental Health Diagnostic Process

While most of us are familiar with the process of diagnosing physical health concerns, mental health is entirely different. It's much more abstract and subjective. There are so many factors that come into play when conducting a clinical interview.

A few of these are:

- The client's ability to articulate their experiences and concerns.

- The therapist being influenced by their training, skill set, competency, personal biases, and trauma history.

- The nature of the human condition. We are not a fixed state. We are multifaceted and will most likely embody many different presentations within a day, a week, a year, and over a lifetime.

Unlike medical practitioners who use X-rays, lab work, CT scans, and MRIs, mental health therapists work with very little concrete data when diagnosing clients.

A diagnosis is one person's opinion based on their limited interactions with the client, alongside the client's self-report.

It is a snapshot in time of what may be a transient state.

People often move through symptoms to the point where they no longer meet the criteria, so this is just a reminder to hold any labels mentioned with a loose hand.

There are also a variety of physical and environmental factors that can contribute to what we call mental health symptoms. I'm including this alongside information on the diagnostic process because, to an extent, it is a process issue. Most therapists do not have the training or tools to screen for physical health concerns prior to making a mental health diagnosis. This means symptoms will most likely be attributed solely to mental health. In many cases, psychiatric medication will be prescribed, all without identifying the root cause. The implications of this are far-reaching and to describe them as alarming is an understatement.

An example is someone who lives or works in a water-damaged building and is exposed to mold. They may tell a therapist they're feeling lethargic, unmotivated, sad for no reason, and experiencing brain fog. If a therapist isn't familiar with mold illness, there's a high likelihood the client will be diagnosed with depression and prescribed an antidepressant. Meanwhile, the root cause has yet to be identified and thus remains unaddressed. Not to mention, the person may have an onset of new symptoms due to the side effects of the medication.

The irony is that by prescribing a pill, the practitioner is acknowledging the person is experiencing a physical concern; however, psychiatric medications fail to address the actual root cause.

I share more about physical and environmental factors that can affect mental health, as well as psychiatric medications, in the next two chapters.

A Few Reminders
<ul><li>Hold symptoms and diagnostic labels with a loose hand.</li><li>Your current presentation is quite possibly a transient state.</li><li>Symptoms are something you're experiencing, not *who you are*. It is a wave, but you are the ocean.</li><li>Do not hesitate to seek a second opinion from someone who is trained to determine and treat the root cause.</li></ul>

Chapter 14

Physical and Environmental Factors That Can Contribute to Mental Health Concerns

If you allow yourself to be present with the idea that physical and environmental factors can present as mental health concerns, you may feel a little overwhelmed at first, but ultimately hopeful. I saw this firsthand in 2019 when I experienced almost immediate relief of histamine intolerance symptoms (anxiety, panic, OCD, brain fog) by implementing a low-histamine diet. While that was a temporary fix, it went a long way to help me function while working with my FMD to determine a root cause. I realized during that time that to a large extent, we've been barking up the wrong tree when it comes to treating mental health.

Physical imbalances—such as brain inflammation, vitamin deficiency, and disruptions in our circadian rhythm—can negatively impact brain function. This can present as anxiety, depression, brain fog, neurosis and rigidity, panic, depersonalization (feeling like you're not real), derealization (feeling like the world isn't real), listlessness and detachment, disorientation, and even psychosis. These symptoms can understandably impact our outlook on life, reactivity to events, ability to complete daily tasks and stick to a routine, mental clarity, and sense of hope for the future.

If we have systemic inflammation and our nervous systems are dysregulated, we are more likely to feel overwhelmed and traumatized by daily life—both by the actual events and the way we perceive them.

Also, I don't want to be dismissive of trauma or insinuate that it alone can't drastically impact our health, but as I discuss in Appendix A, if our bodies aren't strong enough to act as a container for our emotional experiences, then we may find ourselves dealing with physical symptoms as well. The way this can look in the mental health therapy setting is a client with a history of abuse seeks support to cope with her stressful job and overbearing supervisor. She tells the therapist she rarely eats breakfast and has become reliant on caffeine, candy bars, and potato chips to get her through the day. She has also developed a habit of falling asleep shortly after as she gets home from work, often with the television on and without eating dinner. The client expresses concern for her physical health as well, since she is overweight, lethargic, experiences occasional waves of panic, has irregular menstrual cycles, erratic blood sugar, and acne.

If I were the therapist seeing this client, I would be very careful not to downplay her current experience of a toxic work environment and physical health concerns, even if I think the history of trauma and current dietary choices are contributing to her poor health status and workplace challenges. I would work with her to formulate a treatment plan according to her goals, resources, capacity for change and discomfort, and receptivity. I would also refer her to other practitioners to address areas that were outside my scope.

Unfortunately, by the time we reach adulthood, our health concerns are rarely due to only one factor—especially in today's world—so it can be challenging to decide what to address first. Ideally, we would stabilize the physical body before embarking on a mental or emotional healing journey, but sometimes, the body won't let go of a symptom until we address the emotional component.

See below for a list of factors to consider when experiencing "mental" health symptoms:

- B vitamin deficiency
- Histamine intolerance
- Electromagnetic fields (EMFs)
- Lyme disease
- Mold exposure
- Artificial food dyes
- Gluten intolerance

- Structural abnormalities
- Sensory processing challenges
- Retained primitive reflexes
- Heavy metals
- Circadian rhythm disruption
- Thyroid issues
- Hormone imbalance
- Problems with iron metabolism and storage
- General toxicity
- Detox reaction
- Parasites
- MTHFR genetic mutation

This list is not exhaustive. These are just some things I've learned in the past ten to twelve years as I've navigated my own health journey. See Appendix D for more information on each item on the list. I've also included websites and book recommendations in the Resources section if you're interested in learning more.

Chapter 15
Medication and Related Matters

While therapists are not authorized to prescribe medication, they do work directly with clients who are taking them. During my time in the military and in private practice, I saw the following:

- Clients were prescribed a medication that previously gave them negative side effects (including suicidal thoughts) despite sharing their concerns with their physician.

- Insurance companies required physicians to prescribe medications in a certain order and document failed attempts prior to approving other medications. In my understanding, this was due to cost. According to the National Association of Mental Illness (NAMI) website, these practices are referred to as step therapy or fail-first policies.[6]

- Clients missed a few doses of their medication due to difficulty accessing the prescription (for personal or administrative reasons), then had withdrawal symptoms so severe they were hospitalized.

- Clients interpreted acute withdrawal symptoms as their true selves, which reinforced their perceived dependency on the medication.

- The medication acted as a barrier to identifying the root cause of mental health concerns.

---

6. NAMI, "Medications: Step Therapy," National Alliance on Mental Illness, accessed November 6, 2024, https://www.nami.org/advocacy/policy-priorities/improving-health/medications-step-therapy/.

- Each time a new symptom surfaced, the recommendation from the prescribing physician was to "tweak" the meds. Over time, it became very challenging to distinguish between organic symptoms and medication side effects.

- Clients were prescribed additional medication(s) to address the side effects of other medications.

- Clients agreed to use psychiatric medication temporarily, but then were unable to access proper guidance on how to safely discontinue it when they wished to do so.

I wish I could say the above scenarios are rare, but I actually don't believe they are. If I had to guess, I'd say situations like the ones I described are becoming increasingly more common.

Since closing my private therapy practice, I've learned even more about the Western medical landscape regarding psychiatric medications and have heard from several people that doctors have a tendency to downplay the difficulties of tapering off psychiatric medications when recommending them to their patients. Whether this is due to lack of education provided to doctors or a result of the incentives from pharmaceutical companies, patients are not being informed of the risks and side effects of psychiatric medications prior to starting them. As I said in the introduction of this book: true informed consent can only occur in the presence of full transparency.

As a therapist, my hands were tied. It was like watching a train wreck. Because therapists are not authorized to write or adjust prescriptions, the only thing I could do when clients shared concerns about their medication was encourage them to speak with their prescribing physician. If they did not feel comfortable doing so, then that was the place to start. While the client and I could certainly work on assertive communication, address limiting beliefs around having needs and preferences, and explore any barriers they had to advocating for themselves, changes to the medication regimen were ultimately between the client and the doctor. While addressing communication challenges and limiting beliefs with a therapist can be beneficial, it's a lot of work to do just to get what you need from practitioners who are supposedly there to help.

The Zoom-Out Perspective

As I write this, I'm realizing that the situation I described above—and the feeling of helplessness that came from knowing there was very little I could do to help clients with the negative effects of psychiatric medications—is actually a microcosm of the role the *entire* mental health system is playing in society right now.

> **It's as if therapists are supposed to somehow ease the public outcry and help create the illusion that things are improving, but their involvement only serves to make things slightly more bearable in the absence of true systemic change at the societal and cultural levels.**

From this perspective, therapists are the scapegoats—or even the linchpins—of our dysfunctional society, and their attempts to help serve to keep the dysfunction in place. It is in this way that therapists' empathy is being weaponized against them. Their emotional resources are being siphoned and funneled toward an unaccomplishable mission; meanwhile, they aren't given many tools to actually effect change. I can confidently say that no book, class, training, or internship equipped me with what it would take to fix the situation we're in; and it feels really freeing to just be honest about that!

Whether the mental health system was created specifically to enable widespread dysfunction (by appeasing and pacifying us as we cope with a multitude of societal ills) would probably be an interesting discussion with the right group of people, however, having a definitive answer isn't actually required to decide whether it's a good fit for you. Similar to how we can step away from people and relationships without making them the enemy, we can also extricate ourselves from organizations, agencies, and even entire mental constructs without having irrefutable proof of malicious intent.

Speaking of Doctors . . .

As I mentioned before, there are several doctors who have started speaking out about the dangers of psychiatric medications, but there are still so many who turn a blind eye. I've often thought that if the prescribing physicians were the ones sitting with therapy clients for an hour each week, listening to their concerns and hearing what they have to do just to achieve the bare minimum level of functioning, they would probably think twice before taking out their prescription pad.

Similar to the military, the ones giving the orders are not the ones executing them or seeing the ramifications firsthand. If that were the case, maybe things would change. If doctors spent the same amount of time with patients as therapists do, they would have more insight into the daily struggles of someone on psychiatric medications and would learn about the very specific and profound ways people are impacted by the side effects. Assuming these doctors could stay present and adopt a posture of openness and empathy with patients, they would most likely see very quickly that so many of the medications are not only ineffective but also negatively impacting patients in a variety of ways.

For example, a potential side effect of antidepressants is suicidal ideation.

Yes, you read that correctly. A medication prescribed to treat depression has suicidal thoughts listed as a side effect.

See below taken from the WebMD website:[7]

Antidepressant medications are used to treat a variety of conditions, including depression and other mental/mood disorders. These medications can help prevent suicidal thoughts/attempts and provide other important benefits. However, a small number of people (especially people younger than 25) who take antidepressants for any condition may experience worsening depression, other mental/mood symptoms, or suicidal thoughts/attempts.

Remember that this medication has been prescribed because your doctor has judged that the benefit to you is greater than the risk of side effects.

That last sentence is pretty alarming. The doctor has determined the benefit of the medication to be worth someone having thoughts of ending their life and potentially acting on those thoughts?

---

7. G. Karthik Kumar, "Escitalopram (Lexapro) – Uses, Side Effects, and More," WebMD.com, reviewed September 22, 2024, https://www.webmd.com/drugs/2/drug-63990/lexapro-oral/details.

According to WebMD, the other potential side effects of antidepressants are:[8]

Weight gain, trouble sleeping, anxiety, sexual dysfunction, fatigue, increased risk of bruising, nosebleeds, and decreased sodium levels, which can cause vomiting, drowsiness, crankiness, restlessness, muscle cramps, spasms, weakness, seizures, etc.

To conclude, there's a lot to consider when it comes to psychiatric medication. I tried to be very fair and reasonable when writing about my experiences working with clients who were taking them; I just haven't seen or heard many success stories, particularly in the treatment of anxiety or depression. Once again, the decision to take medication is very personal, and I recommend not using this book as your only source of information when making it!

If you're interested in learning more about tapering off psychiatric medication safely, I recommend the work of Dr. Kendra Campbell. She is the founder of Free Range Psychiatry, which is a non-profit organization that helps people identify and treat the root cause of their dis-ease. I've included Dr. Kendra's information in the Resources section at the end of this book.

---

8. Kumar, "Escitalopram (Lexapro) – Uses, Side Effects, and More."

Chapter 16

Concerns Regarding the Accuracy of the Diagnostic and Statistical Manual of Mental Disorders

In addition to what I consider to be limitations of the mental health system's diagnostic process, I also find the primary text used by mental health professionals to be fundamentally flawed. See below for my concerns regarding the accuracy of the DSM-5.

- It is written from an observer's perspective (from the outside looking in), instead of the perspective of the person experiencing the symptoms. The outsider's perspective will always have its limitations. Regardless of how educated and well-researched we are, we can never know 100 percent of what is going on with another person.

- It doesn't allow for the full spectrum of human emotions.

- It doesn't seem to include input from people who have actually experienced the symptoms it describes.

- It assumes that standardization among clinicians utilizing it is possible. Clinicians vary significantly in the questions they ask, the topics they focus on, and where they steer the assessment. Even when mental health assessments are client-centered, clinicians will naturally rate clients' life events and symptoms at different levels of severity. What one clinician interprets as a level 3, another may view as a level 7. This means a person could see three different therapists and end up with three different diagnostic labels.

- It assumes clinicians are infallible, not only in their ability to accurately interpret and apply the DSM-5, but also in their character, judgment, and perspective. It does not account for any projection or misinterpretation from the person assigning the diagnostic label.

- When describing interpersonal relationships, the DSM-5 assumes the other party is stable, moral, and infallible.

- When describing an individual's social behaviors, the DSM-5 assumes that society as a whole is healthy, functional, self-aware, and communicating clearly.

I'd like to share more about the last two items on the list:

1. *When describing interpersonal relationships, the DSM-5 assumes the other party is stable, moral, and infallible.*

The example that immediately comes to mind is the DSM-5 criteria for borderline personality disorder (BPD). In order to meet criteria for BPD, clients have to experience at least five of the symptoms below:

- Chronic feelings of emptiness
- Emotional instability in reaction to day-to-day events (e.g., intense episodic sadness, irritability, or anxiety usually lasting a few hours and only rarely more than a few days)
- Frantic efforts to avoid real or imagined abandonment
- Identity disturbance with markedly or persistently unstable self-image or sense of self
- Impulsive behavior in at least two areas that are potentially self-damaging (e.g., spending, sex, substance abuse, reckless driving, binge eating)
- Inappropriate, intense anger or difficulty controlling anger (e.g., frequent displays of temper, constant anger, recurrent physical fights)

- A pattern of unstable and intense interpersonal relationships characterized by extremes between idealization and devaluation (also known as splitting)
- Recurrent suicidal behavior, gestures, threats, or self-harming behavior
- Transient, stress-related paranoid ideation or severe dissociative symptoms

The behaviors and experiences described in the list above usually indicate that a person has survived trauma—often in the form of abuse—and hasn't been able to access a sense of safety for a prolonged period of time. I personally don't feel it's accurate or ethical to pathologize reactions to abuse (past or present). While I'm not denying that individuals who experience the symptoms associated with BPD could benefit from support, they're exhibiting the behaviors for a reason, and that reason is not that something is inherently wrong with them. While most therapists wouldn't come right out and say that a diagnosis of BPD is negative or something to be ashamed of, the mere fact that it's categorized as a *mental disorder* indicates that something has gone wrong—that this person is not acting in the *correct* or appropriate way.

Symptoms described in the diagnostic criteria for BPD often occur within the context of relationships. Relationships are symbiotic and functional on some level, and we tend to attract what feels familiar to our nervous systems. Notice I used the word *familiar*, not to be confused with *safe*; however, at the body level, it may register the same way. This is often the case with individuals who lacked secure attachment in childhood due to abuse, neglect, or the emotional reactivity of a caregiver. As adults, they can become attached to unsafe people simply because that feels like home. However, if home was not a physically or emotionally safe place, they may find themselves in imbalanced, disrespectful, chaotic, or even abusive relationships.

So when I say the DSM-5 "assumes the other party is stable, moral, and infallible," I mean it doesn't acknowledge the other person's contribution to the interaction or take into account the circumstances surrounding the situation. This is why we can't determine whether someone's behavior is "appropriate" or within an "acceptable range" (terms commonly used in the mental health system). With this being the case, the diagnostic criteria for BPD are irrelevant at best, and extremely harmful at worst.

To clarify, having a history of trauma or abuse is not a necessary prerequisite for experiencing abuse or mistreatment in adulthood.

My goal with this section is to convey the importance of knowing when you're entering a no-win zone, which is when there's not enough information to make a judgment call or you're being asked to make a call that isn't yours to make.

I'll share more about this below!

It's worth noting that assigning a diagnostic label of BPD is not without potential consequences and, in most cases, is unlikely to actually help the client. Because of the stigma that often accompanies BPD, the label can be used to discredit the person and even interfere with them getting help in the future. This is true for all the personality disorders, and as I sit here today, I have to wonder who actually benefits when these labels are assigned. I can't think of a scenario where it is the client.

Telling someone their personality is disordered is shaming, judgmental, and disempowering. It also fails to instill hope or create space for growth and expansion. Diagnosing someone with a personality disorder does not give them a dignified way forward, and unlike a physical diagnosis, which communicates, "This is a condition you have," mental health diagnostic labels (especially the ones used for personality disorders) communicate, "This is who you are."

Sidenote: If you've had challenging experiences with individuals who exhibited traits associated with a personality disorder, this chapter may not resonate at first, and may even be a little triggering, so I want to clarify.

There's a common misconception that by saying, "People who exhibit traits associated with what the DSM-5 refers to as a personality disorder may have unresolved trauma and should be treated with respect when they reach out for help" is to also say, "I condone all the behaviors they've ever exhibited, regardless of any harm they may have caused, and they should be given a free pass to continue all of their behaviors in the future."

This is a false dichotomy that links two (unrelated) ideas and creates a lot of confusion around the actual issue.

These are two separate topics:

1. Helping people heal
2. Holding people accountable for their actions

I am only addressing the first item on the list, which includes describing what can occur in clinical settings when people reach out for help and how to relate to them in a way that increases the chances of a favorable outcome. Helping people heal is a completely different mission than holding people accountable for their behavior.

It is not the mental health system's job to hold people accountable for their behavior or to act as a disciplinarian. The mental health system's job is to help people heal—at least this is what we've been told.

If someone acts in harmful ways toward others, they will mostly likely experience the natural consequences of their actions—possibly in the form of losing relationships or jobs. Depending on the behaviors exhibited and the severity of those behaviors, they may also face legal consequences. Any disciplinary action they face is separate from the healing work they're attempting to do within the mental health system.

Reminders:

- If you feel someone is mistreating you, you are allowed to set boundaries to ensure your emotional and physical safety.
- How you feel in a relationship is enough of a reason to reevaluate your participation in it.
- You do not require a permission slip from the mental health system (in the form of the person being diagnosed with a personality disorder) to adjust your relationship or to discontinue it entirely.
- Feeling disrespected or unsafe around someone is a valid reason for concern, regardless of a diagnostic label.

If clinicians must assign a diagnostic label to clients presenting with behaviors associated with BPD, they may want to consider something in the realm of post-traumatic stress disorder (PTSD) instead. Receiving a PTSD diagnostic label can be validating to people because it serves as a reminder that they have survived something very hard—which may help reduce shame around their present-day challenges.

Unfortunately, there are limited options to choose from when it comes to post-traumatic stress. Previous editions of the DSM included a condition referred to as complex PTSD. Unlike PTSD, the diagnostic criteria for complex PTSD accounted for individuals who experienced a series of traumatic events and had chronically unmet needs *over a prolonged period of time*—as opposed to what is known as single-incident trauma, which is a one-time traumatic event with a clear beginning and end.[9] The acknowledgment of long-term exposure to multiple traumatic events made complex PTSD a better fit for individuals with a history of childhood trauma, such as abuse and neglect. Unfortunately, complex PTSD was not included in the most recent edition of the DSM. The reason given for its omission is that there was not enough evidence that complex PTSD is a separate condition that warrants its own diagnostic code. I disagree, as individuals who have a history of repeated abuse and trauma present much differently than those who experience single-incident trauma with no prior mental health concerns.

According to the current diagnostic criteria, as outlined in the DSM-5, in order to receive a diagnosis of PTSD, individuals must have experienced one of the following:[10]

The person was exposed to death, threatened death, actual or threatened serious injury, or actual or threatened sexual violence, in the following way(s):

- Direct exposure
- Witnessing the trauma
- Learning that the trauma happened to a close relative or close friend
- Indirect exposure to aversive details of the trauma, usually in the course of professional duties (e.g., first responders, medics)

Once again, the list above fails to recognize cases where repeated traumatic events occurred over an extended period of time, such as in cases of child abuse and other forms of relational trauma. This leaves clinicians with very few options to choose from when assigning a diagnostic label and encourages the use of BPD. However,

---

9. Sadie E. Larsen, "PTSD: National Center for PTSD," U.S. Department of Veterans Affairs, accessed November 6, 2024, https://www.ptsd.va.gov/professional/treat/essentials/complex_ptsd.asp.

10. D. G. Kilpatrick, H. S. Resnick, M. E. Milanak, M. W. Miller, K. M. Keyes, and M. J. Friedman, "National estimates of exposure to traumatic events and PTSD prevalence using *DSM-IV* and *DSM-5* criteria," *Journal of Traumatic Stress, 26*, no. 5 (2013): 537–547, https://doi.org/10.1002/jts.21848.

as I mentioned before, therapists may actually harm clients by diagnosing them with BPD, due to the label potentially creating a barrier to therapeutic progress and interfering with clients getting help in the future. Because a diagnostic code is required for insurance coverage, therapists are put into a double bind. To complicate the situation even further, it is not unusual for insurance companies to request more information in the form of treatment records prior to reimbursing therapists. Talk about a no-win situation!

Now that we've covered concerns about the BPD criteria from within the framework of the mental health system, I'd like to make a few more observations from my current vantage point. It's not necessarily that the DSM-5 criteria for BPD itself is problematic, as it's just a list of behaviors, or words on a page. The problem is the way it's used in clinical settings, or even that it's used at all. What I'm sharing here may be a paradigm shift for some, so stay with me!

By conducting an assessment to determine whether a client meets criteria for BPD, the therapist is asking the wrong question. In fact, I can't actually think of anything less relevant to focus on when someone is reaching out for help. This is the equivalent of seeing a person hanging off the side of a cliff and peering over at them (from a position of safety) and wanting to know what kind of car they drive because someone left their lights on in the parking lot. This relates to what I share in Chapter 5 about the therapist job position having two parts: assessment and diagnostic and helping people improve their lives. In my opinion, the latter should always take precedence.

By assessing someone for a personality disorder, the therapist is positioning themselves as the judge of the client's behavior. To once again use the diagnostic criteria for BPD as an example, the word *inappropriate* is included when describing a client's expression of anger. In order to determine whether they meet the criteria, the therapist must enter into the no-win zone of deciding whether the client's behavior is appropriate. In this way, the therapist and client are once again positioned in an adversarial situation (as discussed in Chapter 4), with the therapist relating to the client as if the client were a misbehaving child. This dynamic is not conducive to therapeutic progress for multiple reasons, the primary one being the lack of trust and safety it creates for clients. It also does not allow clients to embody their adult selves, which is required in order for them to heal and move forward in their lives.

Sidenote: If you're reading this and wondering how therapists can help clients without first diagnosing them, you're in the right place!

This relates to one of the core tenets of the Mental Health Belief System that I described in the Introduction. The third point on the list states, "To receive help for mental and emotional concerns, we must first be assigned a label."

While this idea is prevalent in both the mental health system and society as a whole, I just haven't found it to be true.

I believe wholeheartedly that we can help people with their concerns without telling them who and what they are or about a condition they supposedly have. In fact, we do this with friends all the time! The last thing you would do if a friend called you in distress is tell them they have a personality disorder—at least, not if you were trying to be helpful and supportive.

See Appendix E, where I provide a detailed breakdown of the criteria for BPD through an attachment-focused lens.

The last point on my list of concerns regarding the accuracy of the DSM-5 is this:

2. *When describing an individual's social behaviors, it assumes society as a whole is healthy, functional, self-aware, and communicating clearly.*

When I think of the assumptions the DSM-5 makes about the general population's ability to socialize and interact in healthy ways, I immediately think of the diagnostic criteria for autism spectrum disorder (ASD). It is not only extremely one-sided when describing social behaviors associated with autism, it also labels any deviation from what is considered normal as *disordered*. While I understand that autistic people may have a difficult time functioning in various aspects of their lives and may benefit from support (according to their specific needs and challenges), to label them disordered simply because they navigate the world differently is inaccurate and unethical. While it is not my intention to speak on behalf of autistic individuals, I feel pretty safe in saying that many of the challenges they encounter are not actually due to the ways their minds and bodies work, but instead a combination of the way our society is structured and other people's inability to connect with them.

Surely there is a middle ground where we can acknowledge and support people's differences but not label them as disordered because of those differences.

To illustrate what I mean when I say the diagnostic criteria for autism is one-sided and "assumes society as a whole is healthy, functional, and communicating clearly," I've included the section of the criteria for autism that addresses social behaviors and challenges with communication:

- Deficits in social communication, social interaction, social-emotional reciprocity
- Deficits in developing, maintaining, and understanding relationships
- Deficits in social-emotional reciprocity, ranging, for example, from abnormal social approach and failure of normal back-and-forth conversation; to reduced sharing of interests, emotions, or affect; to failure to initiate or respond to social interactions
- Deficits in nonverbal communicative behaviors, facial expressions, body language

With the above list in mind, I'm sharing a few thoughts regarding society's current social landscape.

In my opinion, the vast majority of people are disconnected from themselves and functioning on autopilot, if not a full-on dissociative state. Many hover at a base level of shock, especially after the world events of the last few years. They are operating under multiple layers of societal conditioning and are too busy and stressed to question it. If we closely observe social interactions while out running errands or attending a coworker's retirement luncheon, we may notice that so much of what people are saying is highly incongruent with their body language and full of subtext, which requires us to read between the lines. I've also found that most people lack clarity within themselves and, therefore, cannot communicate clearly with others. Unfortunately, sarcasm, passive-aggressive communication, and double-sided "compliments" have become the norm in many circles. With this as the operating environment, I would not be surprised if autistic people frequently feel as if they're being gaslit or like their perspective is invalidated because so few people have self-awareness or are willing to take ownership of their contribution to interactions. I personally appreciate how straightforward and literal autistic people can be because they mirror back to me where I'm not being clear—both within myself and in the way I communicate.

The point is, many people do not know who they are or how they feel, so to put the onus of difficult interactions solely on one person and label them as disordered for not fully assimilating into an extremely dysfunctional and inauthentic social environment is ridiculous.

As I'm writing this, I'm reminded of the quote by philosopher Jiddu Krishnamurti:

"It is no measure of success to be well-adjusted to a sick society."[11]

Fortunately, there's been an increase in education and resources related to autism over the past few years, yet we still have a lot more to learn. The autism community is vast and encompasses a wide variety of abilities, levels of functioning, support needs, and resources, and there's often a lot of variability even within the same person on the same day.

While it has become popular to say "Autism is a superpower," I find that phrase a little dismissive and somewhat of a bypass. While people who say it are usually well-meaning, the phrase neglects to acknowledge the inherently traumatic experience that is being born into a world that doesn't seem ready for you or that doesn't realize its need for what you have to offer. While many people can relate to this—especially those with super-sensitive bodies and nervous systems—I imagine autistic people feel it acutely on a daily basis in ways that society is just now beginning to understand. My hope is that we can continue learning how to show up

---

11. Jiddu Krishnamurti according to The Foundation Staff, "Regarding the Quote 'It Is No Measure of Health . . .,'" Krishnamurti Foundation Trust, accessed February 10, 2025, https://kfoundation.org/it-is-no-measure-of-health-to-be-well-adjusted-to-a-profoundly-sick-society/.

for the autism community in increasingly competent and compassionate ways going forward.

Quick note on language: I used the terms *autistic people* and *autistic individuals* because the general consensus at the present time is that autistic people prefer what is known as identity-first language (*autistic people*), as opposed to person-first language (*person with autism*).

Chapter 17
Other Forms of Neurodivergence

While we're on the topic of autism, I wanted to mention that it falls under the broad category of what is now being referred to as neurodivergence. ADHD, sensory processing disorder, and dyslexia also fall under the neurodivergent umbrella, due to the differences in brain and nervous system functioning seen with these conditions.

See below for the definition of *neurodivergent* from an article titled "What does neurodivergent mean?" found on a website called Verywell Health:[12]

> The terms "neurodivergent" and "neurodiverse" refer to people whose thought patterns, behaviors, or learning styles fall outside of what is considered "normal," or neurotypical of humans.

These differences exist on a continuum and are heavily influenced by the person's environment. A few areas that are commonly affected are communication, managing sensory input (lights, sounds, smells, textures), organization of information in the brain (memories, dates, facts), and their relationship to structure and having a set routine. Many neurodivergent individuals possess unique skillsets, such as the ability to grasp broad concepts very quickly, synthesize complex information, pattern recognition, and sorting things into categories.

Despite the gifts that often accompany neurodivergence, there are also challenges. Because neurodivergent individuals experience and relate to the world differently than most people, they may struggle to communicate their ideas in a

---

12. Lisa Jo Rudy, "What Does Neurodivergent Mean?" Verywellhealth.com, updated April 18, 2024, https://www.verywellhealth.com/neurodivergent-5216749.

way that others can understand. As a result, they may frequently feel misunderstood and even judged. It is also not uncommon for people with neurodivergent traits to have difficulty with executive functioning, such as time management, planning, completing tasks, organization, and short-term memory (misplacing their phone or keys). They may need to create a lot of workarounds for tasks that others seem to complete effortlessly.

Neurodivergent individuals may also struggle with body connectivity and awareness as a result of decreased proprioception and interoception (defined below).

- **Proprioception:** The brain's ability to sense where the body is in space and its location relative to others.

- **Interoception:** The brain's ability to receive and interpret data concerning the body's internal state. This includes hunger and fullness signals, pain/pleasure sensations, and emotions.

Individuals with neurodivergent traits usually have extremely sensitive nervous systems and can easily become overstimulated. Due to the way their bodies receive and respond to sensory information, it is not unusual for them to exhibit sensory-seeking behavior, sensory-avoiding behavior, or a combination of both (defined below).

- **Sensory seeking:** Seeking sensory input
  Examples: Initiating touch, loud music, attending events where there are large crowds

- **Sensory avoiding:** Avoiding sensory input
  Examples: Preferring quiet music, using earplugs to decrease sounds or tinted glasses to dim bright lights

In my experience, neurodivergent individuals are highly intuitive and energetically sensitive, so they tend to pick up on a lot more than just surface-level material. This can make social interactions exhausting and uncomfortable for them at times because they receive information from others' body language and nervous systems (usually below conscious awareness) yet are expected to just respond politely to what is being communicated verbally. Whether this is because their five senses are heightened or they actually have extrasensory abilities is too individualized to comment on. Regardless, when neurodivergent minds and bodies are constantly receiving so much information, they may present differently than others, struggle to find common ground while socializing, notice details that other people miss, and be ready for a nap by 11:00 a.m. each day!

Fortunately, we've seen an increase in interest and awareness regarding neurodivergence over the past few years, along with intentional efforts to acknowledge and celebrate what is referred to as neurodiversity. See below for the definition of neurodiversity from an article titled "What is neurodiversity?" found on the Harvard Health Publishing website:

> Neurodiversity describes the idea that people experience and interact with the world around them in many different ways; there is no one "right" way of thinking, learning, and behaving, and differences are not viewed as deficits.
>
> The word neurodiversity refers to the diversity of all people, but it is often used in the context of autism spectrum disorder (ASD), as well as other neurological or developmental conditions such as ADHD or learning disabilities. The neurodiversity movement emerged during the 1990s, aiming to increase acceptance and inclusion of *all* people while embracing neurological differences. At the same time, Judy Singer, an Australian sociologist, coined the term neurodiversity to promote equality and inclusion of "neurological minorities."[13]

Those who exhibit traits associated with neurodivergence—especially children—have so much to offer in the way of guidance for the future of humanity. In fact, who's to say they don't contain within them the blueprints for the way ahead? I often wonder if individuals with neurodivergent traits incarnated specifically to push back against the unnatural world we've created and to encourage us to grow and evolve. Just by existing, they invite us to question so much of what we've previously accepted as truth.

---

13. Nicole Baumer and Julia Frueh, "What is Neurodiversity?" Harvard Health Publishing, November 23, 2021, https://www.health.harvard.edu/blog/what-is-neurodiversity-2021 11232645.

I happen to have a few neurodivergent traits myself, and I've realized over the past few years that they are the most evolved part of me. To clarify, I am not saying I am an enlightened guru or ascended master. I'm saying out of *all* the traits, characteristics, and qualities that make up my entire being, it's the ones that are now being referred to as neurodivergent that seem to be the most advanced.

Ironically, it was my tendency toward neurodivergence that made it possible for me to write this book, but also what made the writing process extremely challenging! It is truly a double-edged sword for me. I feel pretty safe in the assumption that I'm not the only one. A common thread among neurodivergent individuals seems to be having extremely defined strengths and weaknesses (meaning we're either amazing at something or terrible at it), whereas the neurological profiles of people who do not identify as being neurodivergent (currently referred to as "neurotypical") may be more balanced.

To use numerical values to loosely illustrate this, a neurodivergent person's functional "report card" may be a mixture of 0's and 10's (on a scale of 1–10), whereas a neurotypical's may have mostly 4's, 5's, and 6's. To further expound upon this hypothetical scenario, some of the areas rated may be creativity, computer skills, information technology, written and spoken language, mathematics, musical talent, artistic ability, building, administrative duties, time management, etc.

In my opinion, we've created a society that overvalues some gifts, talents, and skillsets, while undervaluing others. Because of this, it's not shocking that a large percentage of society is really struggling right now, as I can't think of anything more miserable—or conducive to the onset of "mental illness"—than being expected to perform at a level 8 to 10 in areas that you may naturally perform at a level 2 or 3 in, while having all of your "10" areas downplayed or ignored completely. These are my thoughts after years of seeing myself overachieve in some areas and really struggle in others—as well as (consciously or unconsciously) create workarounds and compensatory strategies to make up for the deficits or weak spots.

With this in mind, it is both for personal and humanitarian reasons that I dream of a world where we understand and respect each other's sensitivities, and where everyone's gifts and talents are valued. When it comes to children, doing everything we can to protect them from the very things that the rest of us are now healing from—particularly physical toxins and emotional trauma—will go a long way toward ensuring they are clear vessels to receive and transmit the information they came here to bring through.

Chapter 18
Ethical Considerations When Assigning Diagnostic Labels

Regardless of anything I share in this section, if we can't guarantee the accuracy of the DSM-5, it is automatically unethical due to how high the stakes are when we're working with people's hearts and minds—not to mention the ways a diagnostic label can impact a person's life. That being said, there is more I'd like to add.

I've already mentioned that the DSM-5 is written from an outsider's perspective, as opposed to the person who is actually experiencing the symptoms.

Why does this matter?

This is yet *another* example of the "doctor knows best" mentality. While I cover this in Chapter 12, I'm addressing it from a slightly different angle in this section.

The emphasis of this chapter isn't on whether mental health professionals have valuable feedback to offer. It's about imposing a perspective onto people who are in a vulnerable state that increases their dependency on the practitioner and system going forward. Another way to say this is "Let me tell you about you." While feedback from a licensed professional may be welcome when we're feeling lost, confused, and disempowered, it's a really fine line. If a doctor or therapist portrays they know me better than I do and that I need them to tell me who I am, and I believe them, I may find myself in a rescuer-victim dynamic or trauma bond, as explained in Chapter 11.

When the client's empowerment and autonomy are the priority, the clinician will naturally and intentionally work their way out of a job. Ethical practitioners are always trying to help clients become liberated and independent, instead of reliant on them.

Chapter 19
Additional Thoughts on the DSM-5

The DSM-5 is a list of behaviors that people can exhibit. If you're seeking assistance with identifying or naming behaviors, it may help you do that. However, while written material can be helpful, it has limitations. It is concrete and stagnant, while life is fluid and ever evolving.

A new friend in Austin, Texas, said it best when we were discussing the application of ideological frameworks to everyday life: "The map is not the territory."[14] The irony is not lost on me that books, podcasts, and blog entries can only take us so far. They can inform the way we navigate the territory, but they will never replace our own embodied experience with the actual territory. While exploring these resources can be transformational, the second we become too dogmatic about the material, we become a slave to it.

Yes, we can actually enter into a trauma bond with a book or podcast!

Now, back to the *Diagnostic and Statistical Manual of Mental Disorders*. Even if we assume that it was written with the purest of intentions, it is still an extremely primitive and antiquated interpretation of human behavior. I joked with a friend that if we found the DSM-5 in the $1.50 box at a yard sale, it may entertain us for half a day. However, it may also send us straight to the bar afterward!

While we may at first be delighted to recognize ourselves within the long lists of human behaviors and reactions, we may also find that shame, disappointment, and hopelessness quickly follow. This is to be expected when we're given detailed

---

14. Alfred Korzybski, "Supplement III: A Non-Aristotelian System and Its Necessity for Rigour in Mathematics and Physics" (paper), presented before the American Mathematical Society, New Orleans, Louisiana, December 28, 1931.

descriptions of our perceived flaws and inadequacies, or when we hyperfocus on the multitude of ways we can "malfunction."

Where is the manual on all the beautiful and brilliant things humans can do and be? Let me find myself within the pages of a book that describes how resilient and adaptable we are, or how being really present with someone during a moment of vulnerability may be the only healing "modality" they need. Perhaps we could even dedicate a chapter to all the things that evoke joy, awe, and wonder, and allow us to transcend our current reality just long enough to access a shift in perspective.

Now, that is a book I'd love to read!

Chapter 20
Potential Benefits of Diagnostic Labels

Regardless of my personal thoughts on the shortcomings of the mental health system and the diagnostic criteria, I realize it's what we have in place for now, and that it's still serving a purpose for some people at various points in their journey. It is for this reason I want to acknowledge the potential benefits of obtaining a diagnostic label:

- Being assigned a diagnostic label can help people understand themselves. It can also help with self-acceptance and reducing shame around the ways they feel different than others.

- Having a diagnostic label can assist in creating a shared language between the client and therapist, and anyone else the client chooses to share it with.

- Diagnostic labels can provide insight into potentially effective interventions, as well as treatment contraindications.

- Being assigned a diagnostic label may result in increased access to resources.

- A diagnostic label may help people find a community of like-minded individuals who are navigating similar challenges.

- Receiving a diagnostic label can help people legitimize their concerns to others. This may be helpful for those who feel invalidated or unsupported by those around them.

- Having a diagnostic label can help people legitimize their concerns to themselves, which may result in increased self-care and making positive lifestyle changes.

- Having a diagnostic label can help maintain the homeostasis of the family system.

You may notice that some of the items listed above are less about medical necessity and more about what can be described as second-order effects. This is what I like to call the functionality of mental health concerns.

I want to share more about a few points on the list:

1. *Receiving a diagnostic label can help people legitimize their concerns to others. This may be helpful for those who feel invalidated or unsupported by those around them.*

As a society, we're operating at a deficit when it comes to compassion, understanding, and even basic kindness. There is a scarcity of humanness. It is for this reason that people may require a label from a clinician just to access the base level of respect or consideration from others, or to be heard or taken seriously.

As I'm writing this, I'm realizing there are two distinct ways this can show up:

- **You must be unwell to secure and maintain an emotional connection.** This could be in the form of a mental or physical illness that results in you being disempowered, and maybe even dependent on the other party.

- **You are not allowed to be unwell if you want to maintain a connection.** In this scenario, your family and friends expect you to function optimally at all times, and there are consequences for (perceived) weakness, such as illness, emotional expression, or needing rest. If you exhibit any signs of imperfection, a diagnosis is required to substantiate your claims.

If you relate to either of the above scenarios, the good news is, you may actually be doing better than you think! However, there's also a chance that you're unintentionally solidifying symptoms by continuing to participate in imbalanced—and potentially harmful—relationships. I've seen firsthand how the body will create whatever is required to get its needs met, including its needs for connection. It's up to you to determine whether those needs are being met and if it's worth the potential trade-off.

2. Having a diagnostic label can help clients legitimize their concerns to themselves, which may result in increased self-care and making positive lifestyle changes.

Oftentimes, the fact that we're struggling isn't enough. We require someone we deem an authority figure to see us struggling and tell us that we are. If this is the case, we may also require a diagnostic label before we address our mental and emotional concerns or implement wellness practices.

3. Having a diagnostic label can help maintain the homeostasis of the family system.

This is what I call functional dysfunction. Frequently, within dysfunctional family systems, one family member has to be unwell in order for the family to feel normal or achieve homeostasis. This is called being a scapegoat or identified patient.

See below for a quote from a blog entry I wrote in early 2022 on family scapegoats:[15]

The Scapegoat is the "release valve" of a toxic family system. Family scapegoats usually have physical or mental health concerns from years of absorbing the disowned shadow material of the family unit. They may feel like the physical embodiment of the dysfunction, a.k.a. the symptom bearer . . . they are the seers in a family that doesn't want to be seen, and they pay the price.

If these dynamics are at play, the family members are most likely trauma bonded to each other and only know closeness through chaos. This is usually not occurring at a conscious level, but it is observable if you know what to look for. These families require a crisis in order to feel close and connected. When someone has a "medical event," everyone plays their usual roles: the rescuer, the caretaker, the entertainer, the advocate, the runner, etc. They know the drill.

It is in this way that mental health treatment—and having an extensive mental health history—can be functional. However, it serves the needs of the family unit, as

---

15. Lindsey Carter, "Going 'No Contact' with Family Members," *Anatomy of an Awakening* (blog), April 6, 2022, http://lindseys-blog.com/2022/04/06/going-no-contact-with-family-members/.

opposed to the health of the individual. Any "love" and belonging they do manage to receive comes at a cost. It is in exchange for being unwell. (Hint: This isn't love.)

I also want to add that obtaining a diagnosis doesn't necessarily ensure that the person will feel seen, heard, and loved by their family, even if it seemed like that would be the case on the front end. Oftentimes, a bait and switch occurs, in which the family invalidates the person's concerns until they produce documentation by a professional, but then the family uses the diagnosis to discredit the person. It's truly a no-win situation.

If the description of the family scapegoat feels familiar, you may benefit from getting support.

However, it's not because you're inherently flawed or defective.

It's because you are worthy of love and belonging that doesn't come at the expense of your health and well-being.

When it comes to recruiting the mental health system to help you address these specific concerns, I'd say it's hit or miss. It depends heavily on the practitioner, as well as their knowledge of, and experience with, dysfunctional family systems. In some cases, the mental health system can exacerbate trauma incurred within abusive relationships and toxic family systems by recreating rescuer-victim-perpetrator dynamics and thus reinforcing the survivor's sense of powerlessness.

The Healing Power of Validation (Including Self-Validation)

As a society, we've been grossly underachieving for so long in the area of mental health education and awareness. Because of this, it is not unusual to hear stories of people who have struggled for years with mental and emotional concerns before finally being diagnosed with a disorder, then experiencing an improved quality of life as a result.

What I find interesting about these stories is that in some cases, the only thing that changed was receiving the diagnostic label. The person's lifestyle basically stayed the same, but yet they seem to be doing much better.

Why is that?

I have to wonder if prior to being diagnosed, the problem wasn't necessarily that the person didn't know what was wrong, it was that their concerns weren't being adequately seen or acknowledged by the people around them—or even *themselves*.

While having our mental health concerns taken seriously by others can go a long way (and may actually be a matter of safety, depending on the circumstances), it's not a replacement for taking our own mental health concerns seriously.

For example, if you know you get anxious in crowded restaurants, have trouble with combat scenes in movies, and need a few days to decompress from social events, it's really important to keep these things in mind when you're planning your week and to do everything you can to set yourself up for success—regardless of whether you've received a diagnostic label (possibly PTSD in this case).

Because we've been conditioned out of having mental and emotional needs from a very young age, it's not surprising we have trouble even knowing what we need, much less taking steps to ensure those needs are met (including communicating them to others).

Speaking of knowing what we need. . .

It's important to identify the specific need you're hoping to meet by receiving a diagnostic label so you can decide if engagement with the mental health system is the best course of action—or if there's a more effective way.

Chapter 21
Potential Drawbacks of Receiving a Diagnosis

Just as there can be benefits to receiving a diagnostic label, there can also be drawbacks.

See below for a few unintended consequences of diagnostic labels I've seen over the years:

- People can become so overidentified with a diagnostic label that it becomes a barrier to healing.

- Receiving a diagnostic label can be traumatic (sometimes more so than the original trauma).

- Being diagnosed with a mental health condition may create or trigger shame and reinforce a belief that clients are inherently wrong, bad, or flawed in some way.

- Having a diagnosis could impact clients' eligibility for certain job positions.

- Receiving a diagnostic label may impede self-exploration, as all signs of imbalance get attributed (or explained away by) the label—regardless of whether the root cause is identified.

As I read this list, I can't help but think of the role that societal stigma plays in how we relate to diagnostic labels. Unfortunately some diagnostic labels are viewed as being less favorable than others. I suspect this has more to do with how the person's symptoms impact those around them, rather than the extent to which they are suffering. It's also easy to overidentify with other people's stories or prognoses who have been assigned the same label (including characters in movies and TV shows).

I want to be really clear in stating that my intentions are not to judge or shame anyone for seeking a diagnostic label. I am no stranger to the fact that life is hard and trauma and mental health concerns are real. That is precisely why I decided to write this book.

My hope is that the information I share will only result in people having *more* support and resources, not less!

Chapter 22

Navigating Discussions Around Mental Health

Disclosing Mental Health Concerns

This section is less about receiving a diagnosis and more about sharing it with others. Unfortunately, some people may view you differently or make judgments based on your disclosure. When this happens, the new perception is often unfavorable. Interestingly enough, this can happen even if their experience of you has been positive. This may point to their concerns being more about the label and their ideas about what that means rather than behaviors you've exhibited or the dynamics of the relationship. I attribute this to the following:

- Portrayal of mental illness in movies, TV shows, and the media
- A lack of knowledge pertaining to mental and emotional health
- Societal stigma around certain mental health conditions
- People's lack of self-awareness or insight into their own challenges
- The tendency for people to defer to a medical professional instead of trusting their own lived experience

It's important to use discernment when deciding who to share information with regarding your mental health. If you aren't sure whether someone has the capacity to be a safe place for your disclosure, you could start by sharing just one or two concerns instead of going into detail about the frequency or severity of symptoms, or using a specific diagnostic label. This will help you gauge their level of receptivity and determine whether to share more.

Learning about Others' Mental Health Concerns

To cover all the bases, I'll flip this around and address it from the perspective of the person who is just learning of a friend's or family member's mental health diagnosis.

When people share about their mental health, on some level, they may be saying, "I'm having a hard time." If your goal is to support them, you could use one or more of the following phrases:

- "I appreciate you trusting me with this. It will stay between us."
- "I'm sorry you're encountering some challenges. I'm here to listen."
- "Let me know how I can support you."

Your presence and *way of being* often speak louder than your words, but having a few affirming phrases on hand can't hurt.

While you may be compelled to share your opinion or ask a lot of questions, this might be a good time to pause and just listen for a few minutes. So often we feel entitled to information about people's experiences or assume they want our feedback, but what they really want is to be seen, heard, and accepted for who they are and where they are on their journey.

Receiving information about people's mental health concerns may feel awkward, scary, or even shocking, especially if you weren't aware they were struggling or if you haven't seen them exhibit what you would consider to be mental health symptoms. It's important to remember that the outside appearance or presentation is only part of the equation when it comes to mental health and well-being. We aren't always given a backstage pass to the person's day-to-day lived reality, and therefore, we can't possibly know what it entails. While someone may appear to be doing fine, only they know how they really feel and what is required for them to function.

If I've learned anything as a therapist and a human, it's that people are mentally and emotionally fighting so many unseen battles that we'll never know anything about.

I also want to acknowledge here that people may be relieved to have a diagnostic label for a variety of reasons. This is why it's important to suspend judgment and refrain from projecting your thoughts and opinions onto them or their situation. Once again, if your goal is to support them, then what matters in that moment is how *they* feel about their situation.

Everyone's relationship to diagnostic labels is unique; therefore, you can't assume the person is upset about receiving one. It is also inappropriate and unhelpful to tell them why you don't think they have the mental health condition they're sharing about. While this may be well-meaning, it communicates that you either view mental health concerns as intrinsically negative or that you don't even believe that they are experiencing concerns. Denying someone's experience—or the way they conceptualize it—demonstrates an unwillingness to see and be present *with all of them.*

Rejecting someone's diagnostic label or denying their experience of mental health concerns seems to convey that, on some level, you want them to hide or suppress their symptoms when they're around you. This may be so that you can maintain the idealized image you have of them, or because it causes you to question things about yourself that you would rather avoid. Regardless of the reason, expecting people to suppress their mental health concerns to make you feel comfortable is asking them to pretend to be someone they aren't. It may also communicate that you're not an emotionally safe person. So once again, it just depends on your goals for the interaction.

To deny someone's whole self creates and reinforces shame for everyone involved.

When we are comfortable with our whole selves, we become a safe place for others to be their whole selves.

I am using the term *whole self* instead of *true self* because it acknowledges the entire person and allows for their fullest expression. I've also learned the hard way over the years that we don't get to choose which version of a person is their true self; only they can decide that.

To conclude: If the idea of discussing mental and emotional concerns with the people closest to you feels stressful, it's probably because as a society we haven't been taught how to navigate sensitive topics or to relate to each other's differences with acceptance, compassion, or even neutrality. Instead, these interactions are often characterized by fear, judgment, and denial.

The way I see it, holding space for others' unfolding, staying present when we'd rather check out, and the willingness to truly see people for who they are (strengths *and* challenges) are the true ninja skills that will help us create the world we want to live in.

Chapter 23

An Overview of Misogyny and Misandry in Healthcare Settings

There has been an adversarial and divisive energy on this planet long before any of us stepped onto the scene, and it is unfortunately still alive and well. This energy is insidious and shows up in nearly every facet of society.

It infiltrates our minds, and walls off our hearts. It locks into our wounds and gets entangled with our identity and our worldview. Once we become a vessel for this energy, we will almost certainly allow it to work through us; that is, until our eyes are opened, and we choose a different way.

While it is a shapeshifter and can take on many different forms, a primary way this parasitic energy expresses itself is through what is known as misogyny and misandry.

What are misogyny and misandry?[16]

- **Misogyny:** hatred of, aversion to, or prejudice against women.
- **Misandry:** hatred of men.

While I was hesitant to speak on the topics of misogyny and misandry—because they are far more complex, nuanced, and situation-specific than I can convey here—I do think it's important to acknowledge how the mental health system can perpetuate

---

16. "misogyny," *Merriam-Webster.com Dictionary,* Merriam-Webster, accessed February 10, 2025, https://www.merriam-webster.com/dictionary/misogyny; "misandry," *Merriam-Webster.com Dictionary,* Merriam-Webster, accessed February 10, 2025, https://www.merriam-webster.com/dictionary/misandry.

each one. While I believe that misogyny and misandry have the same root cause (individual and generational trauma), they manifest in distinctly different ways.

In the next four chapters, I'm sharing how they can show up in the mental health system and in our present-day society.

Chapter 24

The Convergence of Misogyny and Misandry

Before I go any further, I want to point out that not only is there a huge overlap between misogyny and misandry but it's impossible to have one without the other. While I originally set out to address each one separately, it became very clear that the convergence needs to be acknowledged.

To test my theory on the interconnectivity of misogyny and misandry, I viewed each one from several different angles. I started with the requirements for procreation, then considered what I believe to be the ideal conditions for healthy child development. I followed that with the characteristics of strong family units and, finally, the building blocks of functional communities. When exploring each level individually, then zooming out to take in the totality of the situation, I concluded we have a much better chance of experiencing healthy and functional individuals, families, and communities when both men and women feel safe, supported, and valued for their natural gifts and proclivities. Conversely, the devaluation or commodification of one or the other is not without its consequences.

The oppression of women results in children being raised by vacant, disembodied, and dissociated mothers. When this happens, there is a lack of nurturing and attunement. It results in adults who have no tolerance for emotions or discomfort and who self-soothe with addictions of all kinds. The suppression of men leaves both the family unit and the community unprotected and without the masculine container required for safety—both the felt sense of safety and actual safety. Without a grounded and solid masculine presence at every level, there is chaos, confusion, and defenselessness.

When viewed through this lens, it becomes very apparent that misogyny and misandry aren't about men *or* women, but rather all humans. To harm one is to harm all. What is done to anyone is done to everyone. When we buy into the idea that the problem is either men *or* women, we're operating out of separation consciousness. It is a form of scarcity mentality and reinforces the belief that saying yes to you is saying no to me, and that someone has to sacrifice themselves in order to meet in the middle.

Chapter 25
Internalized Misogyny and Misandry

It is a misconception that only men can perpetuate hatred and distrust of women and only women can perpetuate hatred and fear of men. Both misogyny and misandry can be internalized, meaning women can be misogynistic and men can experience misandry.

Internalized Misogyny

Internalized misogyny is when women feel hatred and mistrust toward other women, or even their own feminine nature. For example, there's a common misconception that women practitioners in medical settings always serve as advocates for women. I have often found the opposite to be true. In my experience, many women have had their nurturing instincts weaponized against them and are now working more on behalf of the system than the individuals seeking support from it.

Because women have to work so hard to be heard and taken seriously in male-dominated environments, they are often reluctant to do or say anything that would result in them losing credibility with those in charge (usually either men, or women who are operating in their masculine energy). Because of this, women can be less likely to deviate from the standard protocols—even when their intuition is guiding them to—and more likely to position themselves as the arbitrators of other women and their bodies. An example of this is a woman doctor pressuring a woman patient into receiving a medical intervention that the patient isn't comfortable with. The patient may view the female doctor as more trustworthy than the male doctors, but that is not necessarily the case, due to the reasons I mentioned above.

Another example of internalized misogyny that is prevalent in society is women criticizing other women (or girls) in the areas of appearance, speech, creative expression, and sexuality. Basically, it's women policing each other under the guise of helping them, and it happens all the time. I've witnessed it firsthand, particularly in hierarchical environments such as church, the military, and unfortunately even designated "safe spaces" designed for healing, such as yoga studios, women's' circles, and retreat centers. It is also very prevalent with social media influencers. If these women were asked why they are being critical of other women and young girls, some may claim it's for their betterment, edification, or even safety. However, because criticizing women only perpetuates the control, suppression, and silencing they have endured all throughout history, those who behave this way are actually doing the work of the establishment.

Policing and monitoring others can be a symptom of Stockholm syndrome. My personal definition of Stockholm syndrome is when a person becomes so overidentified or aligned with an authority figure (person or system) that they act to further their (potentially oppressive) agenda. The person will often defend the authority figure, even in the face of evidence that they're acting in harmful or destructive ways. I want to be really clear in saying this behavior is usually a symptom of trauma and abuse, and thus cannot be entirely separated from the environment in which it occurs. When people in oppressive systems feel threatened and interpret there is no way out, their survival instincts kick in. This applies to all people—not just women.

Internalized Misandry

Internalized misandry is when men experience hatred and fear of men, including their own masculinity. One way this can look is a man having shame around his own masculine qualities. This may cause him to disown his masculinity and judge the masculine traits in others. He may hold negative and unfavorable beliefs about men (including himself) and even relate to boys and young men in overly harsh and punitive ways.

An example of internalized misandry is a man who is physically or verbally abusive toward his stepsons and regularly assigns punishments that are disproportionate to the supposed offense. He may have unreasonable expectations of the young boys, in that what he is asking of them is not developmentally appropriate, or it requires a skill that hasn't been taught or explained. As a general rule, we relate to children in the same way our caregivers related to us when we were children, so if this man was punished as a boy for his natural expressions of masculinity, such as playing in the dirt, running indoors, or rough housing with his friends, he may have developed shame around behaviors typically associated with adolescent boys and feel they need to be redirected, stifled, or even punished.

The scenario I'm describing is much different than providing guidance and structure for young boys while teaching them the value of hard work and instilling values such as dedication, perseverance, and integrity. An easy way to differentiate between the two is that the former is done out of anger, impatience, and emotional reactivity, and the latter from a calm, grounded, and intentional place. There is also the question of whether the desired behavior is being modeled by the stepfather to the young boys, or if it's more of a "do as I say, not as I do" situation.

Another example of internalized misandry is a man who was never allowed to express anger as a child and now suppresses his anger as an adult. The result is a passive-aggressive communication style with occasional fits of rage. Meanwhile he is likely to judge and shame men who express their emotions—especially anger.

In Conclusion

Misogyny and misandry can be symptoms of trauma, as we often recreate our traumatic experiences by treating others in the harmful or oppressive ways we were treated, or even unconsciously using them to reenact what was done to us. I believe this is a mechanism of life itself that helps us heal by allowing us to see and experience our internal material in the external world so we can process it and ultimately bring it to resolution. However, if we aren't aware this is happening, we'll just run the program over and over again.

Chapter 26
Misogyny in Healthcare Settings

A pretty strong case can be made that the medical system is structured specifically to disconnect women from their internal guidance and even to convince them they are "crazy." Whether it's with medication that numbs women's body sensations and drowns out their intuition or with therapeutic approaches that perpetuate the following ideas:

- Women's bodies and minds can't be trusted.
- Medical practitioners know best when it comes to women's mental and emotional health.
- Women should adjust themselves to accommodate mistreatment.

The idea that women's bodies and emotions are inherently problematic and need to be fixed is prevalent in all facets of healthcare. It is not uncommon for a prescription or surgical procedure to be recommended as the first line of defense when women seek assistance from the medical system. These interventions are often utilized prior to trying less aggressive interventions—or even attempting to identify and address the root cause.

Sidenote: Medication and surgery may be what some women are seeking when they engage with a medical provider. If that is the case, no judgment! I'm just speaking to the current operating environment and illustrating the value of having a variety of options to choose from.

Because women are often gaslit and dismissed in healthcare settings, being offered any intervention at all may be an improvement over the practitioner denying there's even a concern to address.

One surgical procedure that is frequently performed is a hysterectomy. This is the removal of the uterus and cervix. While it is a major operation that often results in long-term physical and emotional effects, it is often presented as the first option (if not the only option) when women share concerns with their doctors.

Yes. You read that right. After all the technological advances we've supposedly made, the best we have to offer women is to cut it off, cut it out, silence it, make it stop.

My definition of misogyny is the belief that women exist only to serve and nurture others, as opposed to being whole people with their own thoughts, beliefs, dreams, and goals. When misogynistic energy and attitudes are present, women are assigned a function to perform, a service to provide, or a role to play—and if they're unable or unwilling to do so, they're either punished or discarded.

There are consequences for stepping outside the box, and there is often no grace available for failing to live up to the role they've been cast in, or an image others created.

In the medical system, the message still seems to be that women and their bodies are to be seen and not heard. It's as if the system is saying, "If you cause too much trouble, you're out of here." If we truly want to heal what ails us as individuals and as a society, women's health is a good place to start.

By giving women's bodies and minds such a narrow permission field, we've stifled our own life force.

To wage war on a woman's body is to be at odds with life itself, and when we do this individually or collectively, we will suffer.

When I considered specific ways misogyny can show up in the mental health treatment arena, the first thing that came to mind was the tendency for therapists to overidentify with male clients and act to form an alliance with them to the point where it alienates their female romantic partners (in heterosexual relationships). This can occur regardless of the therapist's gender. Misogyny can also show up when therapists encourage women to practice behavior modification to appease or pacify men, or to prevent mistreatment at the hands of abusive partners. These dynamics can occur in couples therapy or individual sessions.

Here are a few examples people have shared with me over the years:

1. **A female therapist in individual therapy diagnosed a male client's female partner (not present in the session) with a mental health condition.**

It is unethical to diagnose or share clinical judgments about people who aren't clients. Even if the person being discussed is a client, disclosing information about them violates the Health Insurance Portability and Accountability Act (HIPAA).

While the client's partner's behavior may be contributing to his concerns, placing the responsibility solely on her prevents him from learning and growing from the situation. As a general rule, therapy sessions should not be centered around *other people's* actions and perceived flaws. It is for this reason that I would be a little wary of therapeutic "progress" that takes the form of "We cracked the code! It's all the other person's fault." This is a little exaggerated to illustrate the point, but you get the idea.

2. **A male faith-based therapist advised a young female client on how to communicate with her abusive boyfriend to avoid triggering him. This included the therapist saying, "Show him more respect," and "Don't overly question him."**

While I'm sure this advice was well-meaning and was given in an attempt to ensure the client's safety, the therapist not only failed to address the actual issue, he focused on helping the client become more skilled at enduring abuse instead of exploring her options for leaving it. The therapist's feedback may have also reinforced any feelings of helplessness and dependency the client had, since it seemed to communicate that the abuse was inevitable and that staying in the situation was her only option.

In my opinion, it would have been a better use of the therapy session—and more helpful overall—to assist her in formulating a safety plan that included alternative living arrangements.

Of course, we can't know the client's goals or assume she wanted to leave her partner, but advising her to become more passive in an attempt to prevent mistreatment is inappropriate and potentially harmful.

3. **A female therapist instructed a woman in couples therapy to comfort her male partner during conflict and reassure him of the stability of the relationship.**

To ask a woman to put her reactions and emotions on the back burner and tend to a man's emotional needs is not only asking her to self-abandon, but it places her in the role of the mother, and the man in the role of a child. Any female therapist who suggests this approach is most likely also playing the role of the mother (consciously or unconsciously) and tending to the male client's inner child.

The idea that the woman needs to reassure the man of the relationship's status in the middle of a conflict is bizarre to me personally. For one, the relationship status may actually be uncertain depending on the circumstances surrounding the conflict, so to suggest that she reassure him of its stability denies the woman of her emotional process.

It actually doesn't help the man either. Instead of him experiencing the fear and discomfort that comes from thinking the relationship may end, he is rescued from those challenging emotions and robbed of the gifts they have to offer him. The irony is that the man's experience of thinking the relationship may end may be the exact catalyst that's needed to shift the course of the relationship.

I would also say that the way each partner conducts themselves during a conflict and the efforts they make to repair any ruptures can be the make-it-or-break-it factor in whether the other partner chooses to continue their relationship. Because of this, they're not always able to say, "Don't worry, it's all going to be okay," or "I'm not going anywhere," because it has yet to play out.

Instructing the woman to tend to the man's emotional needs during conflict is merely a short-term solution, or Band-Aid approach, that most likely stems from the female therapist's inability to tolerate the male client's momentary discomfort. However, it results in stunting the growth of both partners and the relationship as a whole by maintaining a rescuer-victim or parent-child dynamic.

When therapists attempt to rescue men from challenging emotional experiences—or encourage the men's female partners to do so—they are not doing the men any favors. It's reinforcing the idea that men are immature children or inept cavemen who are incapable of taking responsibility for their actions. This results in them feeling just as stuck and disempowered as the women do.

The examples above are admittedly very tricky, as a therapist's primary focus is addressing the client's needs and concerns and helping them reach their goals. If the client's goals conflict with what the therapist believes is in their best interest, the therapist may find themselves in an ethical dilemma. However, they always have the option to refer the client to another therapist if they are unable to help them for any reason.

To clarify, I'm only sharing some things that can occur within the therapeutic setting to further illustrate the limitations of it. As for what or who is responsible for these dynamics, I attribute the majority of responsibility to the system, as opposed to individual therapists. While I believe it is the therapist's responsibility to do their own personal work and be as healthy as possible when working with clients, it is impossible not to perpetuate some kind of dysfunctional dynamic at some point when you're occupying the therapist role. It is truly a no-win zone.

The level of health and productivity of the therapy session cannot exceed the level of health and awareness of the therapist facilitating it. However, because the therapist cannot override the client's goals and has to remain emotionally attuned to them, the therapist can only go so far. So, it is also accurate to say that the health and productivity of the therapy session cannot exceed the level of willingness and receptivity of the client. While I can appreciate the idea that the therapeutic relationship is a dance—a true art and a science—this just feels like a gridlock or a double bind to me.

Chapter 27
Misandry in the Mental Health System

Within the clinical mental health setting, therapists can easily project their hatred or fear of men onto male clients and cause just as much harm as they can when it happens to women.

I listened to a podcast in early 2023 about how the mental health system is quickly becoming a "moral reeducation center."[17] The host was sharing about her experience as a student in a master's-level counseling program that was instructing future therapists to consider clients' political views when assigning diagnostic labels. It was based on the belief that voting for certain candidates is an indicator that someone is mentally unwell.

While that example is slightly different from the picture I'm trying to paint here, it may be in the same realm. This could show up in mental health treatment as therapists using their influence in sessions with male clients to encourage behaviors they believe men should exhibit and discourage the ones they deem less desirable, or even toxic. While doing so would be unethical, I'm sure it occurs more often than we think, even unintentionally.

The full implications of this are concerning, as it would not only be (re) traumatizing for clients, but it also positions the therapist as a gatekeeper to healing modalities, or just healing in general. Meanwhile, the client is held hostage and can only get help if he conforms to the ideology that's being presented. This should go without saying, but clinical settings are not an appropriate place to push personal, political, or religious agendas. The goal is to help people heal, not to convert them

---

17. "The 'Social Justice' Subversion with Leslie Elliott," *The Way Forward with Alex Zec,* January 2023.

into a belief system. Behavior modification techniques are only appropriate when they're in line with the client's goals.

My Experience as a Female Therapist Working with Male Clients

During my time in private practice, some of my most dedicated clients were men, and I do believe I helped them make progress toward their goals. While men can most likely make some headway in addressing trauma and healing inner-child wounds with a female therapist, they may need additional support. On some level, female therapists may represent the mother archetype, and while that may serve a purpose up to a point, the client will (hopefully) outgrow that dynamic and need to differentiate.

If you're wondering why I refer to the therapist as the mother archetype, it's because of the power differential that is inherent in clinical settings. There isn't really a way to escape it. It doesn't mean the dynamic can't be utilized to help clients reach their therapy goals, but I still think it has its limits.

Back to the topic of misogyny and misandry: When I was practicing as a therapist, I constantly had to assess my personal and professional loyalties. In my determination to not perpetuate misogyny by "throwing another woman under the bus," so to speak, I may have failed to support men in the way they needed at times, as it was hard to strike the correct balance.

For example, I remember occasionally feeling like men were seeking validation and approval for their mistreatment of their partners. Sometimes, male clients would tell me about their female partner's inadequacies and shortcomings, seemingly in an attempt to justify their behavior. If I had to guess, I'd say the underlying idea was that if a woman agreed with them or condoned their behavior, then it must be okay. There's also a chance they felt guilty and like they needed to tell someone they viewed as an authority figure what they did—similar to a child who broke a lamp or a church member attending confession.

It was an uncomfortable position for me to be in, as I was not positioning myself as the judge of their behavior (at least not intentionally). I also realized that saying something that even remotely triggered shame may result in them shutting down completely. Because therapy sessions are only fifty minutes long, it was highly unlikely we would be able to process and repair any ruptures (or perceived ruptures) before the session ended. This meant we would end the session on an uncomfortable or unresolved note, which increases the chances the client would not return, so it was just a gamble.

Because of the dynamics mentioned above, being a female therapist providing mental health therapy to male clients often felt like (yet another) no-win situation. When this was the case, I just tried to be present with the men wherever they were in their process. As I'm writing this I'm realizing how exhausting it was to try to balance personal and professional boundaries within the parameters of the clinical setting.

While I believe all types of relationships between men and women can be extremely healing and redemptive and that they can go a long way in helping us become aware of our biases and view things from a different perspective, the difference is the power differential. Friendships and relationships that develop organically may offer more authentic and reciprocal opportunities to heal than professional relationships that we pay for. I attribute this to the absence of the power-over dynamic that adds a layer of complexity in the therapeutic realm.

Some therapists may read this and think I've missed the whole point of therapy—that relational dynamics will naturally show up in sessions and are actually the sweet spot, or the level at which the deepest and most productive therapeutic work occurs. They may feel it's a safe container for exploring the exact dynamics that led the client to seek therapy to begin with. While I understand that perspective, I think the therapeutic setting can be a mind game for reasons I've already shared, and that it can add more work for clients as they try to sort through what's what. As for the idea that it's safe, once again, that depends on your definition of safe.

Back to the topic of misandry in the mental health system: Whether men encounter overt expressions of misandry in the mental health system, or they just find it is not a good fit for them, there are other options.

Thoughts on Men's Healing

While I'm not claiming to be the expert on men's healing, I'm very encouraged to see all kinds of men's groups, retreats, and other healing opportunities being offered in the US and abroad. These gatherings can provide men with a safe place to express their emotions and experience true brotherhood. They may also get to participate in the initiatory rites of passage that are unfortunately missing from today's society. Some of these groups also incorporate work with plant medicines (psychedelics). It's so encouraging to see men stepping up to lead other men in this way, and I think the movement will only grow stronger from here.

The Healing Power of Community

Now that I think about it, healing in a community setting may just work better for all of us. Assuming the community is healthy and functional, we would have a better chance of moving through challenging seasons of our lives in a way that results in obtaining a sense of mastery, acquiring wisdom, and actually seeing difficult situations come to resolution. Healing in community would also remove the us-versus-them dynamic that I mentioned above, which is nearly impossible to avoid in one-on-one settings with power differentials and hierarchies.

Regardless of whether communities are established specifically for the purpose of healing, they can still act as a container—or safe place to operate from—as people engage in more targeted and intentional healing work. Feeling supported and understood can go a long way in creating the safety required to lean into personal growth and transformation.

Chapter 28
Separation Consciousness

For the purposes of this chapter, I'm using the word *separation* to refer to a resistance to unity and cohesion, and having a need to be positioned adversarially. When I use the word *consciousness,* I'm describing a framework or paradigm. Think of consciousness as putting on a pair of colored glasses that alter your whole perception. It's the lens through which you're viewing the world. When we view the world through the lens of separation consciousness, we feel like perpetual victims and like everyone is out to get us. I'll share more over the next few paragraphs, but this is a good place to start.

The irony is not lost on me that some of the stories I shared in this book were experienced and told from a version of separation consciousness. I say this because I experienced and interpreted events as happening *to me,* as opposed to *for me* (my current perspective). While that wasn't intentional, and I didn't view myself as a victim at the time, acknowledging this helps to illustrate an important point:

When we enter into a setting where there is a hierarchy or power differential, the chances of being victimized exponentially increase because, to a large extent, we're forfeiting our autonomy.

How important is maintaining our autonomy? I believe it is extremely important. Without it, we experience powerlessness, hopelessness, and resignation. In fact, it is often the absence of autonomy that makes trauma traumatic. To say this in a different way: The difference between a stressful event and a *traumatic* event is the element of choice. Interpreting that we do not have a choice—or actually not having one—can result in traumatization.

The awareness that we have a choice is what gives us a choice.

Having a choice (and knowing we do) = freedom

Not having a choice (or not realizing we do) = disempowerment and captivity

When it comes to hierarchical structures, the biggest decision we make is whether to enter into them to begin with. Once we enter a system with a hierarchy, we still get to choose how we navigate the environment to an extent, but there are limitations. This applies to people considering whether to engage with the mental health system and to those working within the major systems (medicine, law, finance, etc.).

Any system with a hierarchical structure creates and sustains separation consciousness, or a two-dimensional reality construct.

Simply put, there's a pecking order.

You're either above or below others in the system.

This becomes very apparent when you're working in a hierarchal structure and someone occupying a position above you makes a decision that makes your life more difficult. Depending on the circumstances surrounding the decision, you may feel helpless and like there's nothing you can do about it. There's often no recourse or even a dignified way forward.

I've also experienced firsthand how disengagement isn't always an option when you're working within the systems like it is in environments without a hierarchy or power differential. If others in the system require discord or "drama," they may be triggered by your lack of engagement and initiate a conflict, which is annoying at best.

A quick way to tell if a person—or entire system—is operating within separation consciousness is that the predominant narrative takes the shape of *us versus them*. There's also a high likelihood that one party is cast in the role of the enemy and the other as the victim. Individuals operating from separation consciousness tend to view situations through an extremely narrow lens. It is not unusual for them to only acknowledge two options—it's either one *or* the other—and have very little tolerance for a broader perspective.

Here are a few examples:

- Wrong or right
- In or out
- For or against
- Win or lose

Does this remind anyone else of a gang, a cult, or the Mafia?

Separation consciousness is a fear-based perspective that creates a false dichotomy and leaves no room for nuance.

This is the mentality that created and sustains the matrix—or paradigm—we're currently operating in.

Separation consciousness can be observed in all of the major systems, especially politics. We are given the illusion of choice, but at the end of the day, we're still playing the same game. It is a game with winners and losers, which only serves to keeps us at odds with each other and ourselves. We are given our heroes and our villains. We are told how to feel, whom to hate, and even how to be virtuous (or at least appear that way). This mentality keeps us fixated on the "other" instead of our actual sphere of influence where we can affect change.

It's not necessarily the idea that there are different sides that's problematic, although it is overly simplified. It's the belief that one side is superior to the other— and thus worthy of favor—and that those on the "wrong" side aren't worthy of respect and instead are instead deserving of mistreatment.

I'm not suggesting we never have an opinion or that we operate from complete neutrality at all times.

The invitation is to hold our beliefs loosely without making others wrong or bad, dehumanizing them, or placing them in a category of other people whom we assume think and feel the exact same way.

Black-and-white thinking is a symptom of a highly traumatized nervous system. It can also be an indicator that someone's inner child is running the show. It's not uncommon for people to experience an age regression when they're triggered. If this happens, they will temporarily adopt the inner-child's mindset and worldview. Depending on which developmental stage their inner child is in, they may not have the capacity for abstract thinking, and they'll likely be more emotionally reactive than when they're fully embodying their adult self. It may also be nearly impossible for them to operate without some type of conflict. When things are too peaceful or quiet, boredom ensues. If there's no drama happening, they'll create it.

Did a name or face come to mind as you read that?

If so, there's a high likelihood that person is emotionally immature and displays traits associated with narcissism and a tendency to be dishonest, divisive, and manipulative. If you've ever tried to complete a work project, negotiate a business deal, or finalize a divorce with someone with these traits, you know it can be unbearably difficult and sometimes just not workable. They drag everything out and make the whole thing way harder than it has to be. This is separation consciousness at its finest. When someone is severely under-resourced and can't access a sense of safety within themselves, they try to source it from the external world. This is why it can feel so draining to be around people with narcissistic traits, because (consciously or unconsciously) there's often an energetic siphoning component to the dynamic, which makes it parasitic in nature.

What do narcissistic traits and energetic siphoning have to do with the mental health system?

The mental health system requires our participation in order to survive, but not just any participation.

It specifically requires us to buy into the belief that we are not okay and that we need something from it in order to be okay.

The system feeds off our intolerance for discomfort, the fear of our own minds, and belief in our own helplessness and incompetence. In this way it is parasitic. The irony is that because it needs us, it has to make us believe we need it—but we actually do need it if we believe that we do!

Chapter 29
Calling a Truce

Now, before we get carried away, I'm not trying to create yet *another* split and cast the mental health system in the role of the enemy and portray myself as the hero for informing everyone of how persecuted, victimized, and oppressed they are. We don't need any more enemies, and viewing something as the enemy is not actually required to heal and step into our power.

One way we could neutralize some of the rescuer-victim energy surrounding mental health treatment is to depedastalize the mental health system and the practitioners within it. There seems to be some kind of universal law or observable phenomenon that occurs the second we place anything above us: we then have to wage war on it. In case you're wondering, I have not found it to be a productive endeavor to fight the systems because—you guessed it—it just further solidifies the divide.

Being at war with any of the major systems not only reinforces the separation and the hierarchy, it's also a huge energy expenditure. This is especially true if you're seeking validation from them or asking for permission to do something. In my experience, getting caught up in a battle with a major institution drains valuable resources that can be used elsewhere (health, travel, general life expenses), and is unlikely to yield the desired effects.

**To fight or be in resistance to something is to maintain
the entanglement.**

The only way to truly be free is to reach neutrality.

The one exception is if you sincerely feel that you need to engage with one of the major systems on a deeper level and to turn away from that calling would register as self-abandonment for you. If this is the case, you may need to just let it play out. At the end of it you will at least know you did your best and tried everything, even if nothing else comes of it.

Now, back to the idea of depedastalizing the mental health system: This happens first in our minds, then it ripples out to the physical plane. As we realize the flaws and inadequacies of the system (and the diagnostic process), feedback and documentation from mental health practitioners will naturally be placed within a more appropriate context than when we viewed them as the all-knowing authorities who have the final say.

Chapter 30

Exploring our Relationship to the Mental Health System

This chapter is intentionally abstract. It is an invitation to explore what comes up for you personally around the mental health system, those who seek support from it, and the role the system is playing in our society.

Each section expresses a drastically different idea, so you may want to take a break in between them!

The Mental Health System as a Mirror

The way I see it, the mental health system is mirroring us.

What do I mean by this?

Well, depending on how you look at it, the system is either a direct reflection of our individual and collective fragmentation and brokenness, or it's reflecting our *belief* that we are broken and incomplete. As I mentioned in Chapter 28, the system feeds off our intolerance for discomfort, the fear of our own minds, and belief in our own helplessness and incompetence. As long as we are walking around with these gaping wounds, we're susceptible to outsourcing our personal power and becoming trauma bonded with a practitioner, or the entire system.

Mental Health "Patients" as Scapegoats

This section is an invitation to explore how people who have been labeled as mentally ill may be acting as a scapegoat for the parts of ourselves we're scared to look at.

The members of society who are struggling with their mental health—and have perhaps even been labeled as severely mentally ill—are holding our collective shadow material for us.

They are the symptom bearers of the collective.

The way we treat members of our human family who are suffering says everything about how willing we are to be with discomfort. Our need to "other" them is really our need to avoid our own dis-ease.

The chasm between ourselves and who we view as the most impaired is as wide as the chasm between our conscious mind and our deepest, darkest wound. The extent to which we push them away is the same extent to which we push the most vulnerable parts of ourselves away.

Some of the harshest mental health treatment modalities and most inhumane psychiatric facilities are, on some level, projections of our own internal landscape— meaning that's how we treat the parts of ourselves we don't like or that we have shame around.

We banish these undesirable parts from our awareness and shove them as far as possible into the shadows.

Mental health "patients" are acting as a mirror, but we refuse to look. We turn away, not realizing that they represent the parts of ourselves that are exhausted, in pain, and are questioning if the life we've created is actually working.

We're content to let them be the physical embodiment of our individual and societal wounds as we continue with business as usual. Running ourselves into the ground, overworking, filling our lives with distractions.

Anything to avoid facing the wounded parts of ourselves. Anything to fill the void. Anything to outrun the shadow that threatens to engulf us. It beckons us from the peripheral, from behind the curtain, inside the closet, or under the bed.

What are we scared we'll find if we dare to look?

Is the fear that we won't make it out alive, or that we'll uncover a version of ourselves that's like "those people" "over there"?

Could we turn and look it in the eye?

Can we look "those people" in the eye?

Can we look ourselves in the eye?

Questions for self-exploration:

- How would it feel to befriend the parts of yourself that you've judged, feared, or disowned?
- To shine a light on the dark corners of your psyche?
- To integrate your shadow material?
- What would it take for our communities to make more room for those we've pushed into the peripheral—or banished to the outskirts—due to their perceived deficits and "failure" to play the roles we've cast them in?

The Systems as a Coliseum or Battleground

While writing this book I couldn't help but notice how all the major systems provide a battleground for externalizing—or bringing to life—the war within us. Whether the battle is with our mind, body, or spirit, we have a system for that!

Exploring which systems you have the most involvement with can guide you back to the original fight.

Here are a few examples:

We join forces with the medical system to wage war on our bodies, and partner with the mental health system to conquer our minds. For those needing reassurance of the existence or quality of their soul, there's organized religion, while the legal system offers nothing short of a trip to the top of Mount Everest and back for those needing to prove their innocence.

When viewed through this lens, the systems are actually doing us a huge favor by helping us gain such specific and individualized self-knowledge. I happen to love this perspective because it fits right in with my core belief that *everything is for us*.

Thank you to the systems for helping us learn about ourselves!

Chapter 31
You Have a Choice

If you realize that your relationship with the mental health system is keeping you in a disempowered state or that you're in a trauma bond with it and feel you're being siphoned—either monetarily or with beliefs about your worth, capabilities, and wholeness (or lack thereof)—you have a choice.

You can either engage with the mental health system differently or withdraw your participation altogether. Either one is a step toward empowerment and will most likely feel better to your internal system than engaging with the system unconsciously or on autopilot.

In case you didn't catch that:

Deciding to seek support from the mental health system *after* doing your own research and tuning into your internal guidance still constitutes moving forward in a mindful and sovereign way.

I meant what I said in the Introduction about not telling anyone what to do. Not only is it arrogant and codependent, it also runs counter to my "live and let live" nature. If I could sum up this book—and perhaps my entire life's purpose—in one phrase, it would be: You do you, but know what you're doing!

Chapter 32
Change the System?

While my goal is not to change the mental health system, I have thought about what that may look like. I came to the conclusion that in order for the mental health system to graduate from the two-dimensional paradigm I described in Chapter 28 and operate from an expanded level of consciousness, the power differential between mental health professionals and clients would need to be completely neutralized—as in nonexistent.

To do this would mean to remove any and all authority that mental health professionals have been given. This would allow the hierarchy within the current system to dissipate and would result in everyone involved in it to function as equals (mental health providers, patients, and clients).

The mental health system would become just a group of people who are eager to help others with no strings attached.

Mental health professionals would still get to fulfill their calling of helping others and would of course still be compensated for their time and energy. The people who access support from the system would derive the benefit of healing and creating a happier life without participating in the power differential or hierarchy.

With no authority attached to being a mental health provider, the system would be more likely to attract individuals with a sincere desire to help and with no interest in being positioned above anyone or to be seen as superior in any way.

It seems like a win-win-win to me!

If the idea of removing the hierarchy and power differential makes you uncomfortable, this is your invitation to sit with that.

Chapter 33
The Illusion of Authority

Something or someone only has authority over us if we agree that they do. There are a few exceptions, but much fewer than you would think. The human tendency to view ourselves as either inferior or superior to others never ceases to amaze me. The need for a hierarchy is deeply embedded in our psyches, and I believe it relates to our inner child's longing for parents. I can definitely relate to entering into jobs, relationships, and living situations that offered a perceived sense of safety in exchange for some aspect(s) of my freedom. I was told what to do, given a strict set of rules, or micromanaged in some way. Ultimately, the trade-off wasn't worth it. So, surprise, surprise—I outgrew every single one of those arrangements! I see now that I was susceptible to those oppressive dynamics because of a subconscious belief in my own incompetence, inadequacy, or general inability to handle life.

Speaking of hierarchies and authoritative structures, I was discussing the idea of our current societal "matrix" with one of my Asheville friends a few years ago, and she made a comment that I thought was interesting: "We created it, so we must've needed it for something." It was during a time of increased political polarization and social unrest in the US, and it wasn't unusual to hear people express a desire to dismantle the systems—particularly the medical system. While I understood their concerns, the idea of abruptly demolishing an entire complex that so many people were involved with—and even dependent on—felt stressful, chaotic, and unwise. All that to say, I found my friend's comment to be refreshingly neutral and levelheaded. It was also permission-giving in that it acknowledged that every part of the journey is valid, and that there's nowhere we're *supposed* to be. We are not lost, we are not behind, we are allowed to just be where we are. Our conversation was a welcome reprieve from the intensity of the times, to say the least!

> **Sidenote**: I sometimes wonder if we (the human collective) created the systems just so we could eventually find our way out of them and forge a new path. Perhaps we've given ourselves the opportunity to complete the normal and necessary developmental process of differentiation from "the parent" on a large scale. The result is a sense of accomplishment that comes from knowing we did it all by ourselves—or as a team, rather.

When I use the term *matrix*, I'm referring to a mental construct that takes the form of a web or grid that is superimposed onto our reality. We make it real by collectively subscribing to ideas and beliefs we've been taught about how the world works and our place in it. We bring the vision to life by participating in it and creating a feedback loop by which it is reinforced. In the case of the conversation with my Asheville friend I mentioned earlier, the particular matrix we were referring to was the network of authoritative systems that have seemingly been placed above us (medical system, legal system, financial system, etc.).

Another example of a matrix is the concept of time. If you zoom in or out far enough, time as we know it doesn't exist. It's an illusion of sorts. While we've all probably tapped into the experience of timelessness while being immersed in a creative project, spending time with someone we love, or doing an activity that requires our *full* attention (like surfing or snowboarding) the truth is that in our current shared reality, we still benefit from the structure and the container that clocks and schedules provide. Even if it is a shared delusion, it's working for us!

I would say the constructs we may be outgrowing are the ones having to do with our bodies and minds—both what they are capable of and the potential they have to heal—and the idea that we need to be overseen, micromanaged, and told how to live our lives from an external source. When we are connected to our bodies and tapped into our own internal guidance, it all becomes very clear.

We have access to exponentially more freedom of thought and choice than we have dared to venture into. If you're noticing internal resistance to this idea, it may be a good time to explore that. We have barely scratched the surface when it comes to our organic human potential, mostly because we've bought into so many beliefs around our own limitations. The societal conditioning, programming, and even indoctrination around our inability to think for ourselves and manage our own lives are deeply ingrained into every facet of society that it's hard to know who we would be without these disempowering messages. I'll discuss this more in Chapter 42, but first, a few thoughts on escaping the matrix.

Chapter 33
Escaping the Matrix

With the definition of the matrix being primarily psychological, the phrase "escaping the matrix" takes on a whole new meaning.

We exit the matrix by becoming whole—or by waking up to the wholeness we already are.

We free ourselves by freeing our minds, or deconditioning.

While writing this, I was thinking about the idea of dismantling systems. That's not what I'm trying to do here, but if I were to take my best guess at how to do it, it would be to dismantle the mentality that sustains them. Once you do that, they will either shift or go away entirely, because they're no longer needed. Once again, it's not my goal, but it's interesting to think about nonetheless. If part of you is feeling triggered by the idea of the major systems changing or going away, I want to clarify: As long as there's a need for them, they will be there. I am working at the theoretical level here because I enjoy discussing concepts and ideas. I'm aware that the practical application is quite different. As I mentioned earlier, the map is not the territory! Written material can go a long way in informing how we navigate the territory, but it should not be confused with the territory itself.

Going back to the idea of escaping the matrix, I'm not necessarily saying we need to *escape* anything. My goal with this book is to help us wake up to what we're participating in so we can decide for ourselves if it's actually working.

The way out of victimhood is to take radical ownership of what we're participating in.

Now, as for healing and accessing the wholeness that is already available to us, I'll share in Chapter 37 what helped me. But first comes a chapter on mental health breakdowns. I'm presenting the idea that they can serve as breakthroughs and act as a gateway to our truest selves.

Chapter 34
Dark Nights of the Soul

Ironically, the fear of "going crazy"—which may actually be the fear of being helpless and dependent—is the very thing that keeps us helpless and dependent! We're so scared to lose our minds that we immediately reach out to a practitioner or system to make sure we're okay, which only reinforces the belief that we are not okay.

So much of modern-day mental healthcare is aimed at blocking and suppressing the freak-outs, the meltdowns, the dark nights of the soul, and the episodes, as opposed to providing support and education on how to skillfully navigate them.

This is unfortunate because they can be the gateway to our true selves, a.k.a. a massive awakening.

I'll share more about this below, but first, I want to describe a recent trend I'm seeing in the mental health field that's a little concerning. A few years ago, I became aware of a series of online courses for therapists that teach about the role of spirituality in the mental health setting—specifically how to determine whether someone is experiencing a mental health episode *or* having a spiritual emergence (another false dichotomy). Although these courses may have been created with the best of intentions, I can't help but notice that they are still operating from the perspective of "The practitioner knows best" and "Let me tell you about you."

While I can see how it may be helpful for people to receive education around awakenings if they have no idea they exist, it still feels inappropriate for practitioners to position themselves as the ones who decide who is having one and who isn't. The medical system places science and academics in very high esteem and uses information obtained through those avenues to establish guidelines, create diagnostic criteria, and formulate treatment protocols. While that may be helpful to an extent, it cannot replace the experiential knowledge we gain from our actual lives or by connecting to our internal guidance.

An awakening offers us the opportunity to cultivate a solid relationship with our own intuition. However, when we become overly reliant on a practitioner to tell us we're having one, we are, on some level, asking for permission to listen to ourselves. By doing this, we position the practitioner as the authority on the topic. They will keep taking academic courses on what constitutes a spiritual awakening and what is just a run-of-the-mill mental health episode. Diagnostic criteria will be created, and people will either meet it or not. Does anyone else find this a little unsettling?

The only person who gets to decide whether someone is having a mental health event or a spiritual awakening is the one experiencing it.

I would also say that, to a large extent, all mental health events are awakenings. It's just a matter of being willing to view and interpret them in this way.

Why does it matter that the medical system is now trying to tell people whether or not they're having a spiritual awakening? To define something is to control it. If practitioners present themselves as the authorities on who is having an awakening and who isn't, they're basically saying we need them to grant us our awakening, or bestow it onto us.

Quick recap before we continue:

Breakthroughs are often disguised as breakdowns.

What differentiates a breakdown from a breakthrough?
The perception of the person experiencing it.

What transforms a mental health episode into a spiritual awakening?
The decision to make it one.

What are we awakening to?
Our innate wholeness, personal sovereignty, and the freedom to define ourselves and our experiences in a way that actually serves us and allows for growth and expansion. Our eyes may also be opened to the part we play in creating our own suffering, and how we can engage with life in a more empowered way.

Spiritual awakenings do not have to include burning incense, contacting ETs, or even doing yoga. You are not required to get a henna tattoo, go vegan, or read every book on enlightenment. Contrary to popular belief, there are no mandated classes, events to attend, or ideologies to subscribe to. The way I see it, the fact that we are even on the planet is a miracle, which makes life itself inherently spiritual.

> **Sometimes, the most sacred practice we can aspire to is putting our bare feet in the grass, connecting to our breath, and recommitting to just *being here*.**

I'm speaking as someone who has traversed many dark nights of the soul and various forms of awakening (including those that occurred prior to 2020) when I say that although they may be challenging, they can absolutely have their place. I am a more integrated and authentic version of myself now than ever before, and the life I've created reflects that. However, I'm aware that this isn't everyone's story. The decision to lean into seasons of intense—and often painful—transformation is a deeply personal one that is highly influenced by one's capacity and resources.

See below for a few common reasons why people enter into an awakening process:

- Seeking answers to existential questions
- Enjoy exploring new ideas
- Taking an interest in personal growth
- Health concerns
- Trauma or loss

Although everyone's awakening story is unique, there are some common observable themes. For example, it is not unusual for people to have an increased need for solitude, and a sudden desire to write a lot or study topics of interest while navigating periods of intense personal transformation. This can result in a broadening of their worldview and perhaps even change the way they define themselves. There can also be significant and noticeable shifts at the cognitive level as the person simultaneously reformulates both their internal and external orientation to the world and their place in it. The somatic component is particularly important during this time. The body's push to release emotions via tears and sensations (chills, sweating, yawning) points to its need for catharsis. Some people experience emotional flashbacks, which are the body's way of re-experiencing and ultimately releasing a traumatic event. As I mentioned in Chapter 1, these flashbacks can occur with or without a memory attached. See Appendix A for more on this.

When we can access the support we need and stay reasonably within our window of tolerance, these times of personal transformation can act as a portal to not only our peace but also our purpose.

Because we're conditioned from a very young age to fear our own minds—instead of how to partner with them—we end up structuring our whole lives specifically to avoid "losing it" or "going crazy." Hollywood, with all of its horror stories, has contributed more than its fair share to our fears, but we perpetuate them by suppressing our feelings and refusing to sit with the heavier aspects of life. If I had to put words to the unspoken cultural messaging around emotions, I would say: "Whatever you do, don't go there."

But what if "going there" is the only way to true freedom?

What if living life in avoidance and constantly running from our pain has now become far more damaging?

I suspect that we avoid difficult emotions, unresolved trauma, and entering into periods of intense transformation due to multiple factors, including:

- **It's the way our society is structured.**

  With productivity and financial gain as the top priorities, overextending ourselves is glorified and self-abandonment is rewarded at every turn. We do not give ourselves the time and space to be anything but on our A game, twenty-four-seven, and are forced into autopilot as a result.

- **Mental health practitioners' discomfort in guiding someone through the process.**

  If therapists haven't seen themselves through a dark night of the soul or an awakening, it's unlikely they'll be comfortable with other people's. If therapists have navigated an awakening, they may feel (as I do) that the mental health system often falls short when it comes to providing a safe and supportive container for deep inner work. I'd also say there's a subtle pressure within the mental health system to have a well-managed caseload, which could result in therapists encouraging clients (even unintentionally) to keep a lid on it.

- **It's simply what a lot of people are asking for.**

  Oftentimes, when people show up in a medical setting, it's with the request—or even demand—that the practitioner "make it stop." According to some, you're an effective clinician if you accomplish this, and you're ineffective (at best) if you don't.

This can all get a little tricky in the clinical setting. Therapists may not be comfortable encouraging clients to fully experience the intensity and severity of their symptoms because there's no way to guarantee clients will survive them. It's also impossible to predict what resources will be required.

See below for the top two indicators that a person is outside of their window of tolerance:

- Thoughts of harming themselves or others
- Losing touch with reality (inability to orient to surroundings, unsure of person, place, or time)

These are signs the person may need additional support. It's not a bad idea to formulate a plan to ensure the safety of everyone involved. This could look like deciding who to reach out to if they start to feel anxious or unstable, as well as a few safe places they can go to get rest or feel more grounded.

I'll conclude this chapter with a blog entry I wrote in summer 2023 called "Losing It" Part 2.[18] I wrote part one on October 24, 2022, if you want to read it, but it's not required to benefit from this one:

An open letter to anyone that's experienced a "mental break," "psychotic episode," an inpatient psychiatric stay, etc:

Congratulations. You've passed through the eye of the needle and come out the other side. People have structured their entire lives to avoid the very thing you've survived.

Whatever you call these events, I view them as initiatory experiences- an invitation to be the midwives of our own rebirthing.

The clinical terminology is often shaming when it should be just the opposite. I'd venture to say many clinicians have never experienced an awakening, and may even use their helper/ healer work as a way to ensure they don't.

We've been taught to fear our own minds, that we would surely perish if we explore what's in there, but I've found that the opposite is true: Only by being brave enough to venture into our internal landscape and learn how to navigate what we find there can we actually be free.

*I believe there's a balance between staying isolated and going it alone, and outsourcing our power entirely and acting to numb, suppress, and stifle the whole thing.
. . .because as tempting as the latter option may be, it usually only prolongs the experience and ensures we'll hang out with it for years to come.*

Just like in an actual human birth, we choose our birthing team, including set and setting, the information we let in, and who's allowed in the room!

---

18. Lindsey Carter, "'Losing It' Part 2," *Anatomy of an Awakening* (blog), July 28, 2023, http://lindseys-blog.com/2023/07/28/losing-it-part-2/.

Growth and transformation are usually uncomfortable because we don't know who we'll be on the other side. We haven't met that version of ourselves because they don't exist yet.

We are simultaneously creating and experiencing ourselves at all times . . . so yes to discomfort, awkwardness, and a little confusion, but navigating these experiences consciously can help prevent retraumatization.

I dream of a world where these transitions are as natural and expected as puberty or menopause and where we have enough knowledge and resources to lovingly and skillfully support each other through them . . . and so it is.

Questions to ask while navigating a breakdown or breakthrough:

- Where did the idea originate that symptoms are permanent and that ending up in a psychiatric facility or death is inevitable unless I intervene in some way?
- What do I need to feel safe and resourced enough to embark upon my own personal awakening journey?
- Is there a way to support my mind and body in what they're trying to do while still honoring my responsibilities (work, family, etc.)?
- What is my window of tolerance?
- Is there a way to safely "lose it" so that I can find it?
- What is my capacity for experiencing periods of groundlessness and disorientation?
- Is this a breakdown or breakthrough?

These questions are deeply personal and highly individualized. We get to decide how we conceptualize our experiences and how best to navigate them.

Chapter 35
Our Bodies Lead the Way

Speaking of awakenings, I've come to view the body as the primary driver of growth and expansion. Simply put, it is leading the way when it comes to elevating our consciousness. I can see now that my entire healing journey served as an upgrade on so many levels, and that my body was merely showing me where I was out of alignment or had boxed myself in.

I now view my body's presentation as a transient state that's giving me information about my life or the way I'm showing up for it. My willingness to hear what it is trying to tell me—and adjust as needed—helps it return to homeostasis.

This is an excerpt from a blog entry I wrote in August of 2023:[19]

> *Our bodies are finding unique ways to communicate to us that it's time to level up. They're exhibiting bizarre symptoms that don't fit our previous diagnostic criteria and are resistant to Western medical interventions (physical and mental health).*
>
> *This is a "forced" consciousness upgrade, and it's inviting us to leave our comfort zones when it comes to healing and growth. Our go-to solutions are no longer working, and the people we thought had all the answers, don't—even if they really want to.*
>
> *We've lived too long in self-inflicted prisons and have not given ourselves nearly enough space to explore what we're capable of.*
>
> *Inconvenient truth: Our physical vessels care very little about our loyalty to control-based systems—except to communicate how constricting they've become. They are man-made and don't stand a chance against the force of nature that is the human body.*

---

19. Lindsey Carter, "Evolve or Die," *Anatomy of an Awakening* (blog), August 19, 2023, http://lindseys-blog.com/2023/08/19/evolve-or-die/.

Chapter 36

Returning to Our Roots:
A Note on Holistic Modalities

My broad definition of holistic health is any method, modality, or wellness practice that supports the body in accessing and maintaining homeostasis—ideally without interfering with its natural rhythms and processes. Holistic healthcare treats the whole person and honors the interconnectivity of not only each body system but also the extremely sophisticated mind, body, and spirit convergence. Holistic modalities work with the body's innate healing resources and help to unburden each system so the body can ultimately heal itself.

What is the difference between holistic healthcare and Western medicine? Holistic health practitioners put more emphasis on determining the root cause of symptoms, and are more likely to utilize natural methods to address symptoms. Holistic health practitioners recognize that, in most cases, the use of pharmaceuticals does not result in complete or sustainable healing, and instead tend to focus on supplements, detox practices, dietary changes, and lifestyle modification.

Over the past few years, I've personally noticed a lot more people taking an interest in holistic health. It is quickly becoming common knowledge that it's so much more than essential oils, meditation, and multivitamins. With that as the predominant narrative for so long, it's understandable that people felt triggered and invalidated by the idea of addressing mental or physical health concerns holistically. If they viewed the above tools as the only options, they might have felt like a failure if sniffing a few drops of lavender essential oil didn't cure their PTSD or trying to meditate away a psychotic episode didn't yield the desired effects.

There are two primary misconceptions about holistic health that I feel may be responsible for some of the confusion and resistance surrounding it:

- Holistic practices are only effective as a preventative approach or for extremely mild symptoms, but once you reach a certain "level," the medical system is the only option.

- Addressing our health concerns holistically or with natural remedies is a recent trend.

I address the first point all throughout the book and share my thoughts on the second point below.

Almost every holistic healing modality that's being used today is actually ancient. If you want to learn more about the origins of some of the commonly used practices, I recommend researching Ayurveda, Traditional Chinese Medicine (TCM), herbalism, homeopathy, and indigenous healing practices.

I learned the following in a Pub Med article called "Historical Perspective of Traditional Indigenous Medical Practices: The Current Renaissance and Conservation of Herbal Resources"[20]:

Although written records about medicinal plants dated back at least 5,000 years to the Sumerians, who described well-established medicinal uses for such plants as laurel, caraway, and thyme, archeological studies have shown that the practice of herbal medicine dates as far back as 60,000 years ago in Iraq and 8,000 years ago in China.

Hearing holistic modalities described as "alternative" has just never sat well with me, as I feel the word *alternative* is only used because the Western medical and mental health systems are still viewed by many as the ultimate authority or gold standard. If this perspective weren't so prevalent there wouldn't be the idea that one course

---

20. Si-Yuan Pan et al., "Historical Perspective of Traditional Indigenous Medical Practices: The Current Renaissance and Conservation of Herbal Resources," *Evidence Based Complementary Alternative Medicine 2014* (April 2014): 525340, https://doi.org/10.1155/2014/525340.

of action or treatment modality is an alternative to another one. Instead they would each be viewed as one option out of many, similar to a buffet.

All that to say, if certain holistic approaches or natural remedies seem weird or strange, it's because, as a society, we've been so conditioned to believe that pills and surgery are the only options when it comes to addressing health concerns.

Chapter 37
What Helped Me Heal

Before I share what helped me heal, I want to acknowledge that while I've learned much since 2020, the idea of supporting my mind and body with holistic practices was not new to me. I realized very early on that if I wanted my career in social work to be sustainable, I needed to make self-care a priority.

My interest in health and wellness began as early as high school. Back then, I enjoyed learning about fitness, nutrition, and all types of natural cures. In the years that followed, I read personal growth books, attended group meditation events, and experimented with essential oils. I also benefited from working with practitioners who offered various healing modalities depending on my needs and resources at any given time. These included hypnotherapy, acupuncture, chiropractic care, and even sound healing with crystal singing bowls and tuning forks to balance my nervous system.

It's so funny to look back on now, as most of this occurred during my military career. It was not unusual for me to arrive at the yoga studio in my uniform and leave in flip-flops and a tank top, with my combat boots in hand! Although it may seem paradoxical to some, it was actually the perfect balance for me at the time.

While I greatly benefited from trying each modality, getting to know the practitioners was equally healing. They were brilliant and beautiful people, and I'm still in touch with many of them today. They never seemed to tire of my questions, and they expressed appreciation for my receptivity and willingness to try new things. The point is that I have learned a lot, but not overnight! I know that making positive changes can be overwhelming, which is why I feel called to simplify it as much as I can.

There's part of me that was hesitant to speak about healing because it's so individualized that it's impossible to meet everyone where they are. I'm also acutely aware of the systemic issues affecting accessibility, and even more aware of my own limitations when it comes to changing that. I've experienced firsthand how life can be hard and that even knowing what we need—much less accessing it—can feel insurmountable at times. Despite the challenges mentioned above, and the fact that every person has different resources, advantages, disadvantages, and responsibilities, we're all allowed to share our unique message with the world. While I take complete ownership of my own journey and know that I can't rescue anyone from theirs, I hope to at least help make it a little gentler in some ways. That's why I always try to share what I know about health and healing—possibly to the point of being annoying at times!

I am excited to report that some of the most effective tools were also the simplest and most affordable. While I know there are many supplements, programs, gadgets, and specialty clinics that offer everything under the sun, there's also a lot available to us at no cost. We just may not be taking advantage of it—myself included! It's not that all the gadgets and modalities aren't cool or can't be beneficial in some way, but depending on your goals, I don't believe they're required. So many of the things I see advertised on social media and even offered by wellness practitioners are merely an attempt to rebrand nature and sell it to us in a shinier package. When I speak with someone who wants to improve their health but is concerned about finances, I remind them of all the things we have available to us for free, such as sunlight, grounding, breathwork, physical activity, and fasting.

Our bodies are amazing and contain built-in regenerative mechanisms to help us heal.

Sometimes, focusing on what isn't available can keep us from utilizing the things that are.

Before I go any further, I want to share a list of the tools I found to be the most beneficial to my healing journey.

- Touch for Health Kinesiology
- Myofascial Release
- Acupuncture

- Parasite cleansing
- Bach flower essences
- Colored glasses (chromotherapy)
- EMF mitigation
- Supplements to support my brain and nervous system
- Infrared light panel (brain health)
- Portable sauna
- Facial reflexology (balances the nervous system)

I've used all of the above in various capacities over the past ten to fifteen years, but I've used them more frequently and intentionally since 2020.

When it comes to supplements to support the brain and nervous system, there are a lot to choose from. The following list is not exhaustive, but it may be a good starting point, depending on your current state of health and your goals:

- 5-HTP
- Liposomal GABA
- Phosphatidylserine
- Lion's mane
- Magnesium
- B vitamins

While these supplements may be helpful temporarily, it's really important to determine the root cause of brain and body imbalances. Otherwise, we're merely taking a Band-Aid approach and running the risk of leaving the core issue unresolved. Remember, we can't pull from one area of the body without it impacting another.

As far as other healing resources: I've also benefited from podcasts, social media pages, and occasionally even consults with people whose books I've read or whose social media accounts I follow to get their feedback on a specific topic. I've included several names and websites in the Resources section at the end of the book because there are just too many to list here.

Chapter 38
Thoughts on Accessibility

Oftentimes, when holistic health is mentioned, people ask about cost or mention issues around accessibility. I want to acknowledge this concern, but also challenge it a little.

After taking several weeks to decide how I wanted to approach this topic, I decided to question the idea that physical and mental healthcare is accessible through the current Western medical system. First of all, for accessibility to even be relevant, what the system offers would have to result in an *improved state of health*. As I discussed in the beginning of the book, whether this is the case depends on your perspective and your definition of health. However, if what is being offered isn't actually effective, then having access to it doesn't really matter.

Now, to address actual accessibility. In order for healthcare to be considered accessible, treatment has to be available in a reasonable time frame without people having to jump through hoops, fight insurance companies, and advocate for themselves to the people who are supposedly there to help them. Ideally, treatment would also be offered in a way that allows people to maintain their dignity, and it would not create or reinforce dependency. When people cite cost as the primary obstacle or deterrent to addressing mental health concerns without the involvement of the medical system, they seem to be operating under the following assumptions:

- Mental health treatment is completely covered by insurance.
- Everyone can non-negotiably find a therapist they feel comfortable with, who is also trained in the specific areas they want to address.
- They can see the therapist frequently enough to make progress. (This is dependent on both the therapist's availability and the insurance company.)

If all these were true, then it makes sense that people would be hesitant to leave that and go elsewhere. But if that were actually the case, they may not need to! The reality is that people can't always find a therapist who takes insurance, so they end up paying out of pocket. A quick scan of several therapists' profiles on the Psychology Today website revealed that the current rate for therapy with a fully licensed clinician (not an intern) can range anywhere from $125 to $200 per fifty-minute session. Of course, this can vary depending on location, the therapist's credentials, etc., but it's just something to consider when deciding how to allocate your resources. For example, if you're paying out of pocket to see a therapist and you aren't making progress, you could use the same amount of money to try something different.

The point is, it's important to address any potential illusions and distortions head on in order to make grounded and informed choices about our health. Once we have the facts straight it becomes a lot easier to conduct a cost-benefit analysis and adjust course as needed!

Chapter 39
Health as a Personal Responsibility

While we're on the topic of accessibility and insurance coverage, I'd like to pose two questions that have the potential to be a little triggering. I'm going to ask them anyway and trust we will all be fine!

- Who is actually responsible for our health?
- What role should the major systems play (if any) in the care and keeping of our physical vessels?

These questions are multifaceted, and the answers will be different for everyone, but I started thinking about them really seriously in 2019 after several years of paying out of pocket for treatments that weren't recognized by the medical system as being legitimate or necessary, but they turned out to be the only interventions that actually made a difference. I didn't decide to make my health one of my top priorities because I was trying to make a statement or be trendy, cool, or crunchy. I made health my number one priority because I needed to be well, and the medical system (military and civilian) weren't able to determine the cause of the symptoms I was experiencing.

I credit the above experiences for helping me take full responsibility for my health and basically live my life as if the medical system did not exist. This was the only way I could access a sense of safety in the world. I needed to know that I had my own back as much as possible because I'd seen time and time again that the safety nets the various systems claimed to provide had holes in them!

Chapter 40
A Gentler Approach

I'm of the belief that healing doesn't always have to be as hard as we make it out to be. While healing can certainly be complex and layered, it's a misconception that it has to be as difficult and painful as the original trauma or injury.

This is really important, so I'm going to say it again in a different way: Yes, healing can be frustrating and challenging at times, especially when we're addressing both mental and physical health. In fact, I have often described my own mind-body-spirit situation as a tangled ball of yarn! However, I think there's a lot to be said for accepting that it can be hard but also leaving room for it not to be.

We don't have to match the level of suffering that we've already experienced in order to get well.

Deciding to improve our health and emotional state can actually be the perfect opportunity to practice self-kindness, which in some cases, may be exactly what our minds and bodies are requesting of their owner. Healing can be gentle and compassionate, and sometimes, allowing that to be the case is half the battle. So, while I acknowledge it can be tough, I want to instill a little hope and proclaim that sometimes it's not! We occasionally stumble upon the exact right practitioner, modality, or resource at just the right time, and it just all works out, so it's important to leave room for the possibilities.

Sometimes all that's required is the willingness to let things go. I'm not being dismissive at all when I say this either. While I have seen firsthand how trauma is held in the body, both the mind and the body take cues from each other. Therefore, the *willingness* to release our mind-body-spirit burdens (and the stories we've created around them) can go a long way in moving the needle forward. Conversely, our loyalty to pain and suffering—while understandable—may be the very thing that's standing in the way of experiencing the life we want.

The collective consciousness is expanding, meaning people are waking up! There has never been more awareness or resources than we have now. Gone are the days when we required seven years of Freudian psychoanalysis while lying on a couch and talking to a "shrink" before making any progress. We are smarter and quicker than we've ever been, and we are capable of condensing five years of personal-growth work and mental health education into a single meme or social media video clip.

I'm not trying to rush anyone but rather convey that the current conditions are conducive to healing, growth, and expansion.

You're allowed your process, but just know there are no requirements for the duration or intensity, and you don't get a gold star or extra points for making it harder.

It's so easy to become addicted to our traumas and dramas, the labels, the suffering, and even to healing itself. We can even use healing modalities to shame and punish ourselves. When we engage in wellness practices from a place of impatience or aggression, we may unintentionally solidify our symptoms by creating even less safety for our bodies than they've already experienced. Similar to fighting a battle in a war zone, I'm convinced that friendly fire cuts much deeper than shots fired by the actual enemy we are guarding against. This is how it feels to our bodies and minds when we relate to them in forceful or self-punishing ways. As it turns out, what they teach in the military about never leaving a fallen comrade also applies to ourselves.

When we can access both self-compassion for everything our minds and bodies have been through, and gratitude for their refusal to give up on us, we can partner *with* them instead of leaving them to fend for themselves on the battlefield.

With this partnership as the foundation for our healing journey, we are well on our way to experiencing the wholeness and sovereignty that is our birthright.

Chapter 41
Questioning the Sustainability of Our Modern World

While some would say we're in a physical and mental health crisis, I like to think of it as a revolution. As I discussed in Chapter 34 (on breakdowns and breakthroughs), both can be true. Turns out, intense periods of transformation aren't limited to individuals; society also experiences them, along with the entire human race and even Mother Nature herself! Regardless of whether or not we refer to our current situation as a crisis, we can probably all agree that there's an intensity to these times, even on seemingly uneventful days. While many factors come into play, I believe one of the biggest contributors to our current state is the way our society is structured and what is required of us to continue living in it.

How can we actually have an honest discussion about health when so often we have to dissociate from our bodies and numb our minds in order to function?

So many of the mental health symptoms we experience are actually adaptations to our fast-paced, consumer-driven, workaholic lifestyles. Because the adaptations are still serving us, they will most likely continue. It is for this reason when we don't feel well, we reach for a pill or an invasive procedure, as opposed to exploring the root cause or taking the time needed to truly recover. I remember very clearly during my most acute period of illness my biggest fear was not the discomfort of the actual symptoms, nor the idea that I would be alone forever—or even that I would die.

It was that I wouldn't be able to work.

Think about it. If we didn't have the pressure of getting back to work as quickly as possible, the way we relate to our bodies and minds would look quite different. I don't blame people for not enthusiastically diving into the deep end when it comes to physical or emotional healing, because it's impossible to know for sure how deep it is.

When I tap into the collective energy right now, I feel like we're all aware of a giant tsunami wave that is just barely being held back by a dam that has seen better days. We seem to know intuitively that what we've created is not sustainable, and that it's all feeling increasingly more fragile as time goes on.

It is for this reason I often contemplate questions such as:

- What exactly was the original blueprint for humanity?
- How have we wandered so far from our natural state?
- Are we actually more advanced than previous generations?

When I think of the most natural environment we could live in, I picture either an off-grid community somewhere in the US or a tribal setting in a jungle or rainforest overseas. While I don't believe the immediate implementation of this is required to be well—humans are adaptable, after all—I do think we can learn a lot from exploring how it might look.

The first thing that comes to mind is that most of the "work" we would do would be directly related to survival, instead of all the manufactured busy work we've somehow created for ourselves in our modern-day society. We would also have more time for rest and spending quality time with each other. Within the context of a supportive community, there may naturally be more acceptance of the life and death cycles of the Earth and our species, and less effort and energy put into avoiding or interfering with them. Once again, whether any of us ever experiences a community like I'm describing, exploring what it could be like can go a long way in helping us locate our own version of true north when we feel we've lost our center.

In the absence of real-life opportunities to prove ourselves (whether that be going through rites of passage, or hunting and growing our own food), we lack a stable base from which to navigate the world. We not only have no confidence in who we are, we don't really know if we'd actually survive without the complex—but in some ways, overly comfortable—world we've created.

I predict that in the near future, we will realize the true cost of outsourcing the care of our bodies and minds, and will start taking steps to get reacquainted with the parts of ourselves that we've handed over.

Whether we're talking about healing our communities, our families, or ourselves, the task may seem less daunting when we view it as the journey home.

Chapter 42

Our Natural State

Humans: Who are we?

What would our species even look like if we weren't interfered with at every turn, starting in utero? How would we be different if we were never told that we were inherently wrong or bad, charged money at every turn for water, electricity, and the air we breathe . . . If there weren't constant attempts to create division among us by highlighting our differences and instilling (or installing) fear and distrust?

I am of the belief that if we were allowed to live freely—instead of being thrown into survival mode in multiple ways from a very early age, then indoctrinated with all kinds of societal programs—we would exhibit the following characteristics as part of our natural state:

- **Kindness:**
  This is a natural result of having our needs met and feeling internally resourced.

- **Creativity:**
  Ideas would naturally flow through us. We would know intuitively which ones to cultivate and how to prioritize what's coming through.

- **Wholeness:**
  Without the personality fragmentation caused by trauma, there would be fewer internal battles, very little confusion, and clearer communication.

- **Resourcefulness:**
  We would know how and where to source sustenance and tend to our basic primal needs (food, water, shelter, and human connection).

- **Confidence:**
  We would know who we are and be connected to our internal guidance.

- **Embodiment:**
  We would feel safe enough to actually stay in our bodies instead of dissociating or vacating. Our bodies would feel like home.

- **Attuned to our bodies' messages:**
  We would know what our bodies were trying to tell us. We would be able to interpret symptoms when they occur, if not before.

- **Relational:**
  In the absence of unresolved trauma acquired within our closest relationships we would naturally desire connection with others.

- **Awareness of beauty in the world:**
  As we affirm beauty in others and in the external world, our own beauty would be mirrored back to us.

- **Connection to our basic innocence and innate goodness:**
  If we truly grasped our own innocence, we would not feel ashamed or have a need to project our internal separation onto the external world. We would understand that our inherent goodness is not merit-based or something we earn—rather, as one of the gifts of being in physical form.

- **In tune with nature and its rhythms:**
  We would instinctively follow nature's cues. We would eat foods that are in season, become more introverted during certain times of the year, detox our bodies at other times, honor and prioritize women's cycles, be in tune with the weather patterns, and have balanced circadian rhythms. We would also be less likely to overextend ourselves or push past our bodies' limits.

- **Sovereignty:**

  Personal sovereignty (self-ownership) is not something that an authority figure bestows upon us, nor do we acquire it outside ourselves. It is a birthright that we were granted, along with our breath, when we incarnated here.

This list is not meant to shame humanity for where we're at, or even to say where we should be. Rather than presenting these characteristics as the ultimate goal—or as another thing we need to exert effort to achieve—I'm calling attention to the fact that we would most likely have more consistent access to these qualities without the battle wounds we've all sustained by this point in our lives.

Chapter 43
An Overview of My Current Perspective

As a general rule, the human experience is meant to be witnessed, allowed, and supported, as opposed to analyzed, dissected, and pathologized.

I've seen how taking an overly compartmentalized and myopic approach to health concerns can cause us to miss the big picture and the totality of the person—as well as the interconnectedness of all the parts. In other words, we miss the forest for the trees.

Speaking of trees, this reductionist approach is similar to taking a hatchet to individual trees in an attempt to understand and quantify the forest until we no longer have one. I highly suspect that the need for control is behind the tendency to do this, but here's the thing:

The human body and mind are extremely powerful. They will not be controlled.

They are wild and feral, and they will have the final say.

We cannot escape them, and any attempts to do so will likely result in, well, the situation we're in right now.

I feel that it would be a much more productive use of our time and resources to learn how our minds and bodies work so we can accommodate them. Let the body lead the way. Allow it to tell us how it would like to be supported. I believe symptoms are messengers that can point us in the direction of our truth when we're willing to listen. In my experience, once the intent is met, symptoms will often subside on their own.

The mental health system and the diagnostic criteria utilized within it is one perspective out of many. It is not the final authority on the human condition, nor is the DSM-5 an encyclopedia of health and well-being. The majority of the time, we participate in mental health treatment voluntarily. We choose to show up in a clinical setting, engage with a licensed practitioner, and be assessed and evaluated through the clinical diagnostic lens. If it does not work for us for whatever reason, we can leave and find something that's a better fit.

At the present time, the mental health system is still functional on some level. It's what we have for now. The systems in place will always be a reflection of our current level of consciousness. As we evolve, so will they.

With this in mind, I like to say, "We are where we are because of where we are."

Conclusion

As I sit here today, I can look back on the journey and see how things unfolded in the perfect way, ultimately for my highest good. I actually believe that on some level, I called it all in.

Although there are parts of my story I wouldn't wish on anyone, I also recognize I wouldn't be who I am without them. That being said, I don't think everyone needs to experience everything I did. I believe we get exactly what we need in order to heal, but that by doing a little personal work on the front end and navigating life with a higher level of consciousness, we can create a gentler reality.

At this point, you may be asking, "What happens now?"

That's completely up to you!

I've included a list of resources in the back of the book, and I'm always sharing observations, epiphanies, and personal experiences in the blog. If you're interested in learning more about any of the topics I discussed here, or would like support in applying some of the ideas to your own life, I recommend scheduling an individual coaching session. This will allow me to provide feedback based on your specific concerns, resources, and goals.

Writing this book has truly been an honor and a privilege. Despite the long hours, notes scribbled everywhere, backspacing a million words, and clocking way too much screen time, I'm so grateful I decided to answer the call and embark on this journey. The "birthing" process required that I excavate even more of my own internal material to ensure I stayed true to the message. It invited me into a deeper relationship with myself and helped bring closure to a very difficult period of my life.

It is my sincere hope that this book serves as a catalyst for self-exploration, and that reading it broadened your perspective in some way. I'm reminding myself that this is not the end of the conversation but the beginning—and that the sky's the limit on where we go from here.

Appendices

Appendix A: Aspects of Health Defined

- **Mental health:**

  The state of our internal world.

  Examples: Thoughts, perceptions, outlook on life, coping strategies, defense mechanisms, attachment styles, relational patterns, and internalized beliefs about ourselves and the world.

- **Physical health:**

  Symptoms experienced through the physical body.

  Examples: Headaches, broken bones, allergic reactions, food intolerances, digestive concerns, menstrual irregularities, blurred vision, etc.

  In addition to the symptoms listed above, I'm including a few others that are often viewed as mental health, but usually have a physical root cause: brain fog, racing thoughts, anxiety, depersonalization, depression, sleep disturbance, panic, etc.

- **Brain and nervous system health:**

  A component of physical health, but specifically the brain, spinal cord, and nerves.

  This includes specific areas of the brain and their functions, along with the autonomic nervous system states (sympathetic and parasympathetic).

  Examples: Memory loss, challenges with executive functioning, confusion, inability to recognize faces, poor reading comprehension, focus, etc.

Emotional and mental health will affect physical health, and physical health will affect emotional and mental health. While they can be discussed and addressed individually up to a point, they are ultimately not separate from one another.

This means each symptom is a gateway or entry point into the whole. An imbalance in one area affects the entire system.

If you're finding it hard to understand why I've categorized anxiety and panic as physical health concerns (instead of mental health concerns), let me offer a personal example. Because my body, brain, and nervous system are much healthier than they were following the event in 2020, I can bring to mind the *exact same* thoughts and ideas that resulted in panic back then and have no body response. This illustrates that a thought without a corresponding bodily sensation is merely a thought and would not be considered anxiety or labeled a symptom.

Although I've done a lot of personal work on the mental, emotional, and physical front since 2020, I can say that navigating life with a healthier physical vessel is a drastically different experience. I don't even feel capable of throwing myself into the anxious state that was my baseline for so long. If our bodies, brains, and nervous systems are healthy, we are pretty resilient.

If you want to experiment on yourself, drink two Red Bull energy drinks in the morning and see how many "emergencies" you have before lunch! It's not always this cut-and-dried, but considering these factors is a great way to get to know our bodies and minds, and it goes a long way in building our self-care repertoire or tool kit.

When discussing the mental, emotional, and physical overlap, we have to take into consideration what I call the total body burden. This includes emotional trauma, physical toxins and chemicals, dietary triggers, EMF (from cell phones and Wi-Fi), etc. In addition to coping with the stress and exposures of daily life, our bodies accumulate toxins and trauma imprints in tissues and the fascial system. The fascia is our physical and emotional shock absorber. It protects us by encapsulating anything it deems a threat (including foreign invaders and difficult emotions). It doesn't take long for all of this to add up! If fascia is restricted, the brain-body signaling is disrupted, so we feel numb, detached, and disconnected. Restricted fascia also prevents muscles from activating and deactivating properly and impairs the lymphatic system. The more I learned about the fascial network, the more I realized how emotional wounds can quickly become physical, and vice versa.

In addition to the structural effects of stress and trauma, there are hormonal effects to consider. If we are constantly triggered by a stressful work environment or unsafe relationships, our adrenaline and cortisol levels will be through the roof and will course throughout our entire system until they plummet. With this as the operating environment, it's only a matter of time before we experience signs of burnout and depletion.

Systemic inflammation includes the brain and can either directly impact or overwhelm it by bombarding it with alert signals from the other body systems.

We can also stress out our systems with our perceptions of the world. If we view the world as unsafe and think everyone's out to get us, our body will be in a hypervigilant state at all times, as if it's anticipating an attack. If this is the case, I would still place thoughts and perceptions in the mental health category, and I would put sweating, anxiety, and insomnia in the physical health category. What starts as a thought (mental health) often becomes a physical health concern, and in order to feel better, we'll probably need to address both. By the time it gets to the physical health level, it can feel like a vicious cycle and we can spin our wheels trying to figure out what came first: the chicken or the egg. It seems most people don't pay attention until they experience physical symptoms that interfere with their daily lives, so they end up experiencing both emotional and physical discomfort.

As you can see, it is challenging to separate the mental and emotional body from the physical body. This is why modalities such as acupuncture, Touch for Health Kinesiology, Myofascial Release, and chiropractic care can be so helpful when we're aiming to balance the entire system.

Keep in mind: Any intervention is an interruption.

Any time we intervene, we're interfering with what the body is trying to do, or the "track" that's it's on. While interventions can be beneficial, it's important to do your research and use discernment when deciding which practitioners, techniques, and modalities to partner with to address your health concerns.

Appendix B: Releasing Trauma

Emotions are most intense when they're on their way out. They surface to be released. Try to let the sensations pass through you without overidentifying with them and pulling them back in.

Panic attacks and emotional flashbacks are often the body's way of releasing trauma; however, they can quickly become their own trauma because having such strong sensations can evoke a sense of helplessness. Panic attacks are miserable and potentially debilitating. They can feel like a tsunami of energy randomly overtaking us, resulting in hypervigilance in an attempt to avoid or at least predict the next one.

Because we're rarely taught about panic attacks or emotional flashbacks, they can be accompanied by feelings of confusion, and even betrayal. If we are told anything about panic attacks, it's usually explained with a sense of urgency and can take the form of "Act quickly or it will get worse." With this belief being held so tightly by the majority of the population, it's not surprising that people choose medical intervention in the form of psychiatric medication. Unfortunately, doing so can interrupt and suppress the body's natural process and may even prolong symptoms in the long run.

In my experience:

- **We often start releasing trauma once we access a sense of safety.**
  It is counterintuitive, and I admittedly wasn't prepared for it when it happened a few years ago, but it makes sense. When else are our bodies and nervous systems going to do this? Certainly not while we're in survival mode! As I became more skilled at moving through what I now refer to as emotional clearings, I was able to witness the intense sensations, ground myself, and allow them to pass. Another way to describe this process is "See it, feel it, let it go." This was only possible after I put some things in place to support my mind and body (listed on next page).

- **There are ways to support our systems through this process while still allowing them to do what they're trying to do.**

  During this acute period, I found the following helpful: adding red meat back into my diet (ideally organic and grass-fed), using Bach flower essences, and using a liposomal GABA supplement that came in a little pump bottle and was very fast-acting.

In retrospect, the fact that no one seemed to know what was going on—much less how to help—added to the trauma of that time period. It's easy to see how people reach out for support, only to be met with other people's fears and projections, then end up feeling worse than before. While friends and family may be well-meaning, their feedback may not be helpful and can compound the trauma of these stressful occurrences—especially if they lack personal experience with panic attacks or emotional flashbacks. When this happens, things can quickly snowball. Before you know it, everyone is freaking out, and the situation seems to warrant drastic measures.

Having a broader perspective and expanded consciousness while navigating acute symptoms is everything. My hope is that education and resources will be more available in the future, with this book being one of them!

A potential way forward:

Doing everything we can to create a life where feeling safe is our baseline and feeling unsafe is a rare occurrence.

When we feel safe, we're able to move through strong emotions in real time, as opposed to vacating our bodies and requiring they act as shock absorbers. If we can consistently access this level of self-ownership and embodiment, we can prevent the accumulation of stress and emotional energy that has to be released later. This would help us feel lighter and freer in our bodies and more present in our daily lives.

Appendix C: Survival Responses Explained

In the face of real or perceived danger, we usually default to one of the following survival responses, depending on what our system deems the safest in the moment. This is determined by our biological wiring, societal programming and conditioning, trauma history, etc.

- **Fight:** Engage with the threat. Defend your stance or territory. This is the most confrontational of the four.

- **Flight:** Get out of the situation. Escape any way you can. If you can't physically leave, then mentally check out.

- **Freeze:** Shut down in the face of a threat. Think of an animal in the wild playing dead to avoid a predator. Despite how individuals in "freeze mode" appear from the outside, they are actually in an overactive nervous system state. After all, how calm can you really be with a coyote considering you for lunch?

- **Fawn:** Befriend the threat. This is when we people-please and act overly agreeable in the face of a power differential. In an attempt to stay safe, we may self-abandon and do or say things that are not in alignment with the truth of who we are.

In my opinion, all four survival responses are dissociative states. Any time the true self steps back and the false self moves to the forefront, we're experiencing a form of dissociation. The alternative is to stay fully present and embodied. When we're able to do that, we don't need to resort to the survival responses.

Appendix D: Physical and Environmental Factors That Can Impact Mental Health

This list is not exhaustive. It's a starting place for you to do your own research. On this side of my journey, I can see how so many of our health concerns can be traced back to toxicity (physical and emotional) because of the burden they place on the entire system. The way I see it, the majority of the symptoms listed below are just different ways for the body to communicate that it's at capacity.

If you are experiencing physical or mental health symptoms, it may be helpful to explore the following:

- **B vitamin deficiency:**
  B vitamin deficiency can contribute to a wide variety of symptoms, such as exhaustion, anxiety, hair loss, and histamine intolerance. To the extreme, it can even present as symptoms associated with schizophrenia.[21]

- **Histamine intolerance (HI):**
  Histamine intolerance is the term for the body's inability to regulate and metabolize histamine. HI is frequently an indicator that the total body burden of trauma, toxins, and stress is too great.[22] Heavy metal toxicity and iron overload can be underlying factors in HI.

  Histamine intolerance is worsened by high estrogen, dehydration, and B vitamin deficiency. It can result in chemical sensitivities, gastrointestinal distress, panic attacks, hives, swelling, fluid retention, and symptoms commonly associated with OCD and schizophrenia. Histamine intolerance may be more severe at certain points in a woman's cycle due to its relationship with estrogen.

  To self-assess for histamine intolerance, I recommend trying a low-histamine diet for twenty-four to forty-eight hours. Observe how you feel during this time and take note of any changes in symptoms, including skin, digestive, mental clarity, energy levels. Fasting and colon hydrotherapy may also help to mitigate some common sources of histamine and identify a

21. Dr. Jockers, "B Vitamin Deficiencies: Symptoms, Causes, and Solutions," drjockers.com, accessed November 6, 2024, https://drjockers.com/b-vitamin-deficiencies.

22. Dr. Jockers, "Are You Suffering From Histamine Intolerance?" drjockers.com, accessed November 6, 2024, https://drjockers.com/suffering-histamine-intolerance/.

baseline. Taking DAO enzyme may also help, as our bodies use DAO to break down histamine.

- **Electromagnetic fields (EMFs):**
  EMFs are found anywhere there is electricity. One main type is radio frequency (RF). It is a form of radiation and can have harmful effects on the body. Due to certain devices producing higher levels of EMF than others, and some people's bodies being more reactive to it, this is not a one-size-fits-all topic.

  EMF sensitivity is also referred to as electrohypersensitivity and can result in anxiety, insomnia, nausea, and symptoms associated with PTSD. People with heavy metals in their bodies may be more susceptible to electrohypersensitivity.

  Here are a few ways to decrease your exposure to EMFs: Put your phone on airplane mode at night and when you're not using it, unplug the Wi-Fi router anytime it's not being used, switch to hardwired internet instead of Wi-Fi, and sleep as far away from your home's smart meter as possible. Depending on where your home's meter is, you may want to consider shielding the RF it emits or have the meter replaced with an analog meter. Your electric company can provide information on replacement options.

- **Lyme disease:**
  Tick-borne illnesses can result in a wide range of symptoms due to the systemic inflammation that often accompanies them.

  A few common symptoms are food intolerances, brain fog, exhaustion, depersonalization (the feeling of not being real), derealization (the feeling of the world not being real), pain and soreness, insomnia, panic, weight loss, night sweats, nightmares, chemical sensitivities, and electrohypersensitivity.

- **Mold exposure:**
  In my experience, mold exposure can result in feelings of sadness and hopelessness, lethargy, decreased motivation, flat affect, dizziness, headaches, and disorientation. To the extreme, mold exposure can be disabling depending on the type of mold, how sensitive the person is, their health status prior to the exposure, and the duration and severity of the exposure. According to an article by Dr. David Jockers, people can also

experience sneezing, coughing, congestion, watery and itchy eyes, postnasal drip, wheezing, and itchy throat.[23]

- **Artificial food dyes and processed foods:**
Ingesting artificial dyes can negatively impact the brain and nervous system, as well as gut health. This can result in hyperactivity and inattention, emotional dysregulation, and gastrointestinal distress.

- **Gluten intolerance:**
Gluten intolerance can manifest in a variety of ways, but a few common symptoms associated with it are systemic inflammation (including the brain), anxiety, hyperactivity, inattentiveness, hyper emotionality, low mood, feelings of sadness, obsessions, and compulsions.

  For individuals who are gluten intolerant, skin contact constitutes exposure, and may result in a reaction.

- **Structural abnormalities:**
Oral ties (tongue and lip), forward head posture, and restricted fascia often go hand in hand, and can result in impairment of the lymphatic and glymphatic system, vagus nerve impingement, digestive concerns, sleep apnea, and difficulty breathing.

  Because forward head posture restricts the airway, it can signal danger to the body and activate the fight-or-flight response. If this becomes chronic, it can result in challenges with executive functioning due to low oxygenation of the brain.

- **Sensory processing challenges:**
Difficulty with sensory processing can occur for multiple reasons, including damage to or interference with the cranial nerves. This can result in a tendency to become overstimulated by the environment due to sound and light sensitivity.

  This may result in sensory-seeking or sensory-avoiding behaviors or a combination of both (described in Chapter 17).

- **Retained primitive reflexes:**
Integrating primitive reflexes is an important part of child development.

---

23. Dr. Jockers, "Mold Allergy: Symptoms, Testing and Natural Treatment," drjockers.com, accessed November 6, 2024, https://drjockers.com/mold-allergy-symptoms-natural-treatment/#comment-2435313.

Unfortunately some children do not properly integrate these reflexes for a variety of reasons (physical or emotional trauma or other interruptions to their developmental process). Retained (unintegrated) primitive reflexes can cause difficulty with focus, executive functioning, balance, posture, and regulating the stress response ("fight or flight").

The good news is, primitive reflexes can be integrated at any point in the life cycle—even well into adulthood!

- **Heavy metals:**

  Heavy metals are found in vaccines, some types of fish, and amalgam fillings. Heavy metals can cross the blood-brain barrier[24] and affect the twelve cranial nerves. The cranial nerves are responsible for eye movements, facial expressions, and the ability to taste, smell, hear, and swallow.[25]

  Among other concerns, having mercury in our bodies may result in a lithium deficiency. Lithium helps regulate mood and sleep and is often prescribed for bipolar disorder. If someone is deficient in lithium, they may become very dysregulated and have trouble sleeping. Addressing the heavy metals may be a more effective course of action than relying on lithium long-term (even lithium orotate nutritional supplement).

  For more on the effects of metals in the body, I recommend the book *Crooked: Man-Made Disease Explained* by Forrest Maready.

- **Circadian rhythm disruption:**

  An imbalanced circadian rhythm can contribute to difficulties with sleep, weight management, hormones, and mood dysregulation.

  One component of healing our circadian rhythm is morning sunlight exposure. Morning sunlight sends signals to the entire body that it's daytime, which initiates a cascade of hormonal processes required for optimal functioning.[26]

- **Thyroid imbalance:**

  Thyroid imbalances (overactive or underactive) can present as depression,

---

24. Forrest Maready, *Crooked: Man-Made Disease Explained* (Create Space Independent Publishing Platform, 2018): 355-366.

25. Maready, *Crooked*, 47-49.

26. carriebwellness, "Circadian-Friendly Fasting . . .," Instagram.com, June 11, 2024, https://www.instagram.com/reel/C8FiToqOTkp/?igsh=a2E4Nm91aGNnbzl5.

anxiety, weight gain, hair loss, fluid retention, panic attacks, inability to regulate body temperature, brain fog, exhaustion, and hormone imbalance.

- **Hormone imbalance:**
  Imbalanced hormones are a symptom (not a root cause) and can be an indicator of toxicity in the body. Oftentimes, it is heavy metal toxicity, as the metals tend to settle in the bones and joints and can interfere with thyroid functioning. Having imbalanced hormones may result in mood dysregulation, weight gain, trouble with sleep, irregular appetite, fluid retention, irregular periods, etc.

- **Problems with iron metabolism and storage:**
  Elevated stress hormones can cause the body to store iron in the tissues, causing iron overload in the body and iron deficiency in the brain. Because iron is stored in the tissues, it doesn't show up on blood tests. This leads to people being diagnosed with iron deficiency and advised to take iron, which makes the situation worse.

  Problems with iron metabolism cause oxidative stress in the body and can present as low testosterone, insulin resistance and blood sugar dysregulation, metabolic damage, symptoms associated with autism, and hypermobility—just to name a few![27]

- **General toxicity:**
  It's a common misconception that you have to have acute, dramatic, and memorable toxic exposures to have toxins in your body. Unfortunately, we accumulate them simply by being on the planet. I don't know anyone who wouldn't benefit from implementing a few detox practices from time to time, especially if they're already exhibiting symptoms. A few affordable and accessible ways to detox are infrared saunas, dry brushing, fasting, ionic foot baths, and castor oil packs. It's very important to drink plenty of water and make sure your drainage pathways (skin, bowels, etc.) are open and functioning properly prior to beginning any type of cleanse.

  Depending on your goals, there can be a specific order of operations, as well as contraindications, when it comes to detoxing, which is why I recommend working with a practitioner. One thing I learned the hard way,

---

27. I learned about iron metabolism from a series of conversations with health coach Eric Levinson of Naturally Connected Life. Eric's website and blog can be found in the Resource section at the end of this book.

when we detox, we don't know what we're mobilizing! Our bodies do a great job of storing toxins away from our vital organs (often in fat cells), but when we start provoking them, all bets are off!

- **Detox reaction:**
  Detox reactions can be the result of our drainage pathways being blocked and our bodies being at capacity. They can also be an indicator that we're reacting to the toxins we're mobilizing.

  Detox reactions can occur as the result of embarking upon a detox or cleansing protocol and mobilizing toxins. However, they can also occur when we make other lifestyle changes, including adopting a whole-food diet, incorporating more movement into our day, or trying a new supplement.

  The sky's the limit here, but a few common detox symptoms are headaches, nausea, vomiting, fatigue, and brain fog. A receptionist at a holistic health clinic once told me she hallucinates bugs when she detoxes her liver!

  Anytime I've experienced detox symptoms, I've benefited from drinking more water, taking a binder (such as activated charcoal), and using my infrared sauna. Colon hydrotherapy may also help, but it's important to do your research and find a skilled and trustworthy hydrotherapist who has safety precautions and hygiene as their top priority.

- **Parasites:**
  Parasites are not a root cause. They are the clean-up crew. They show up on the scene to help the body process metals and other toxins. Although their relationship with our bodies is initially symbiotic, they often get out of hand.

  Parasites can deplete neurotransmitters (including dopamine) and produce toxins, such as ammonia. Parasites can interfere with central nervous system functioning and can settle into any body system (digestive, reproductive, etc.) and cause problems.

  There's a little controversy around parasites in the holistic healing world, as some practitioners advise against parasite cleansing and instead recommend building up the body so it can balance the parasitic load on its own. While I understand this perspective, I seemed to benefit from systemic parasite cleansing over a year and a half. I feel it reduced my body's toxic burden so it could more effectively allocate its healing resources to the places it needed them the most.

If I had it to do over again, I would address my iron levels (mentioned above) before targeting parasites, but I didn't learn about problems with iron metabolism and storage until recently. If I'd addressed the iron dysregulation first, the parasites may have balanced out on their own. This is why determining the root cause of health concerns can save time, money, and prevent unnecessarily taxing our bodies (detox is stressful).

To my knowledge, Western medicine is still downplaying the ways parasites can negatively impact our health or denying their existence altogether. It's not unusual to hear in medical settings that people in the United States don't need to worry about parasites because they're a concern only in third-world countries, but I just haven't found this to be the case.

If you're interested in learning more about parasites, Dr. Jaban Moore is a great resource. He has an active social media presence and has a growing team of practitioners at his clinic in Missouri called Redefining Wellness. He is also a Cellcore practitioner, which is a supplement line with cleansing protocols for targeting many different types of parasites in nearly every body system.

- **MTHFR:**

MTHFR stands for methylenetetrahydrofolate reductase, which is a genetic mutation that can contribute to the following: impaired detox pathways, increased risk for miscarriages, increased risk for mental health concerns, trouble with methylation, inability to convert B vitamins (and a tendency for them to build up), and increased risk for adverse outcomes from medications and anesthesia.

The MTHFR gene isn't especially rare, but it is extremely varied in its expression, depending on multiple factors, such as stress, trauma, and toxicity. Individuals with the MTHFR mutation are either heterozygous (one mutation) or homozygous (two mutations). As a general rule, the more mutations you have, the more likely you are to be impacted by the mutation and symptoms associated with it.

While I'm not one to overidentify with any single genetic mutation, in my opinion, MTHFR is an important mutation to know if we have it. Not only can it affect health in very specific and concerning ways, but the solutions can be relatively simple to implement! Over the years, practitioners and online sources (articles and forums) have taught me that living a very clean lifestyle and supplementing with the correct form of B vitamin (methylfolate) and avoiding folic acid are at the top of the list when it comes to mitigating potential challenges associated with the MTHFR genetic mutation.

I highly suspect that people with MTHFR are at a higher risk for vaccine injury due to impaired detox pathways. Vaccines contain heavy metals (mercury and aluminum) and other toxins, such as formaldehyde. While these substances are not beneficial for anyone, individuals who have difficulty detoxing may be more likely to experience adverse reactions—or to experience signs of vaccine injury earlier or more acutely than those with optimized detox pathways.

I learned from a practitioner a few years ago that the MTHFR mutation can be associated with midline defects, such as tongue-ties and cleft palates. With this in mind, I have to wonder if our world's increased stress and toxicity are partially responsible for what seems to be an increase in babies being born with tongue and lip ties (due to the MTHFR genetic mutation getting "switched on"). Just a thought!

Keep in mind, all of our genes work together like a symphony, so what matters most is the body's overall balance. People can live their entire lives with a genetic mutation associated with a certain health condition, but they may never experience symptoms. However, in today's fast-paced world, where it's hard to avoid toxins and stress, being proactive by adopting a clean lifestyle can go a long way.

Working with a functional medicine practitioner can be helpful in treating or preventing health concerns. The practitioner will most likely want to run a few tests, which could include a hormone panel, hair tissue mineral analysis (HTMA) for heavy metals, general blood work, and a full thyroid panel. Depending on the results, the practitioner may recommend nutritional supplements. While I would say that relying on multiple supplements for an extended period of time may indicate that the root cause of symptoms isn't being fully addressed, I have personally benefited from quite a few supplements over the years, especially while navigating transition times or periods of high stress.

Appendix E: "Borderline Personality Disorder"

See below for my breakdown of the DSM-5 criteria for borderline personality disorder through an attachment-focused lens.

- **Chronic feelings of emptiness**

  If we lacked nurturing, attunement, safety, or stability in childhood, we may not feel as if we have a strong sense of self. As a result, we may experience our internal landscape as a void. Feelings of emptiness can vary in depth and intensity, depending on several factors, including but not limited to the circumstances surrounding childhood neglect and abandonment, whether we experienced other forms of abuse, and our present-day support system and resources.

  Developing a sense of self requires experiencing safety and stability in our formative years, which just wasn't consistently available for so many people. The sensation of emptiness is often passed down from previous generations, especially if there was a pattern of parentification (when adults look to children to meet their physical or emotional needs).

  I highly suspect that feeling empty or interpreting an inner void is more common than what is being discussed. Most people stay very busy doing anything they can in an attempt to numb or fill the space.

  A few years ago, I jokingly described this phenomenon as a "pain hole" while talking to a friend on the phone late one night, and he knew exactly what I meant. I'd recently done some healing work with my own pain hole and found that, for me, it was more about being uncomfortable with the feeling of spaciousness than it was about feeling actual pain. I felt too vast, which did not feel safe at the time. I wanted to have a more solid constitution, like the people I viewed as being more well-adjusted to life on this planet! At some point, I had an epiphany: The spaciousness is where our light and divinity reside. Ever since then, I've had more peace around my internal landscape and the way I relate to it.

  My descriptions may be a little too abstract for some, but they helped me conceptualize what I was feeling at the time.

- **Emotional instability in reaction to day-to-day events (e.g., intense episodic sadness, irritability, or anxiety usually lasting a few hours and only rarely more than a few days)**

  If we have unresolved trauma, it is not unusual to be triggered by life events, especially when interpersonal relationships are concerned. Intense emotions are also one way the body releases trauma from the nervous system, as I described in Appendix B.

- **Frantic efforts to avoid real or imagined abandonment**

  When we were children, abandonment could equate to death. Not only did we require love and connection to live, but if we weren't accepted by the tribe or were shunned by a caregiver, we may not eat! Therefore, even the threat of abandonment can register as a life-and-death situation to our bodies and nervous systems.

- **Identity disturbance with markedly or persistently unstable self-image or sense of self**

  As children, we naturally looked to our family of origin and our environment to discover who we were and to develop a sense of self. If our caregivers were emotionally dysregulated, or had fragmented personalities from their own trauma, there's a high likelihood they projected their shadow material onto us. This means we were forced to hold (or represent) the parts of them that they disowned.

  Because we were so vulnerable as children, and our brains and bodies were still developing, there's a high likelihood we internalized the projections and accepted them as our identity. If our caregivers were unstable and chaotic, we may have been viewed as the best, the worst, amazing, terrible, perfect, then evil—all before lunchtime. I wish I was exaggerating, but when you're dealing with emotionally immature people—whether it's due to their actual age or arrested development as a result of trauma—it is not uncommon for them to view you in whatever way serves them the most in that moment.

  When I think about self-image, it reminds me of my own experience of not recognizing myself in the mirror following the trauma described in Chapter 1. It is always possible that people are having a similar experience due to brain inflammation or other physical imbalances. However, over the past few years, I've noticed that when I'm in tune with someone, I can see and feel when one of their protector parts steps in (the ones I mention in Chapter 8). When people adopt those little personas, their body language changes, along with their voice, and they speak from the perspective of the part. So, it makes sense to me that people with childhood trauma have a heightened sense of both their and others' protector parts but aren't always able to decipher what they're picking up on, because it can be so overstimulating and confusing.

- **Impulsive behavior in at least two areas that are potentially self-damaging (e.g., spending, sex, substance abuse, reckless driving, binge eating)**

  The behaviors described are all ways people attempt to regulate their nervous system and manage their internal state. The behaviors can serve as protector parts, and to the extreme, may also be a dissociative state. Simply put, the true self steps back (or vacates), and the protector part moves into the forefront. It's not always the most effective strategy, but it usually serves a purpose in the moment.

- **Inappropriate, intense anger or difficulty controlling anger (e.g., frequent displays of temper, contant anger, recurrent physical fights)**

  Once again, this goes back to nervous system regulation, which can be extremely difficult for those with a history of abuse and trauma.

- **A pattern of unstable and intense interpersonal relationships characterized by extremes between idealization and devaluation (also known as splitting)**

  If our primary caregivers were fragmented, we also had to split off in order to attune to them. This creates fragmentation in our system as well and is known as developmental or relational trauma.

  Once again, we attract what feels familiar to our systems, so it's not unusual to find ourselves in relationships with people who exhibit the same traits as our caregivers or whose nervous system feels similar to ours. These people will inevitably trigger us and activate our survival responses and protector parts. It may be extremely challenging to discern what exactly is happening as both parties' protector parts become activated.

A note on idealization and devaluation ("splitting"): As children it would have been destabilizing to realize that our parents were unsafe, unfit, or unstable, so instead, we may have done "mental gymnastics" to convert them into what we needed them to be. This can continue into adulthood as we put people up on a pedestal, but then have trouble integrating new information that would make them no longer perfect in our eyes. It's like toggling between two different realities.

- **Recurrent suicidal behavior, gestures, threats, or self-harming behavior**

  This relates to the "pain hole." Suicidal thoughts and actions are often a protector part that steps in when the person is outside their window of tolerance.

  Viewing it in this way may help to work with the part, but it doesn't necessarily decrease the intensity of the sensations or completely mitigate the risk that the person will harm themselves.

- **Transient, stress-related paranoid ideation or severe dissociative symptoms**

  If we've been in relationships with chaotic, fragmented, and narcissistic people, it makes sense we would have trouble trusting others. Plus, as I've discussed throughout this book, we tend to attract people who feel familiar, regardless of whether they're actually safe. It's also worth mentioning that what looks like paranoia from an outsider's perspective may actually be our intuition alerting us of legitimate concerns.

  Dissociation can happen for many different reasons and can be very scary. In addition to the reasons I've already mentioned, it can occur when we are gaining insight into our protector parts for the first time—particularly when we start to feel them moving to the forefront. As previously discussed, dissociation can also have physical root causes as well, so it is best addressed on an individual basis.

  To learn more about developmental trauma, I recommend Alice Miller's book *The Drama of the Gifted Child: The Search for the True Self.*

Resources

See below for a list of holistic healing resources.

Brain, Body, and Nervous System Health

People:

- Dr. Jaban Moore:
  https://www.redefiningwellnesscenter.com/
- Irene Lyon:
  https://irenelyon.com/
- Dr. Michael Trayford:
  https://apexbraincenters.com/
- Eric Levinson:
  https://www.naturallyconnectedlife.com/pages/health-coaching
  https://www.naturallyconnectedlife.com/blogs/blogs?page=1

Relationships and Personal Healing

People:

- Dr. Nicole LePera, the Holistic Psychologist:
  https://theholisticpsychologist.com/

Books:

- *The Drama of the Gifted Child: The Search for the True Self* by Alice Miller
- *Silently Seduced: When Parents Make Their Children Partners* by Dr. Kenneth Adams
- *The Empath's Survival Guide: Life Strategies for Sensitive People* by Dr. Judith Orloff
- *The Highly Sensitive Person: How to Thrive When the World Overwhelms You* by Elaine Aron

Psychiatric Medication

People:

- Dr. Kelly Brogan:
  https://www.kellybroganmd.com/
- Dr. Kendra Campbell, Free Range Psychiatry:
  https://freerange.org/

Books:

- *A Mind of Your Own: The Truth About Depression and How Women Can Heal Their Bodies to Reclaim Their Lives* by Dr. Kelly Brogan

Circadian Rhythm/EMF

People:

- Carrie Bennett:
  https://www.carriebwellness.com/
- Sarah Kleiner:
  https://sarah-kleiner.mykajabi.com/

Books:

- *The Invisible Rainbow: A History of Electricity and Life* by Arthur Firstenberg

Modalities:

- Touch for Health Kinesiology:
  https://touchforhealth.us/
- John Barnes Myofascial Release:
  https://myofascialrelease.com/
- Neuro Acupuncture:
  https://www.neuroacupunctureinstitute.org/
- Internal Family Systems:
  https://ifs-institute.com/

Wellness products:

- Infrared sauna
  Therasage: https://therasage.com/

- Infrared light
  GembaRed: https://gembared.com/
- Blue light-blocking glasses
  Bon Charge: https://us.boncharge.com/
- Ionic footbath
  Ion Cleanse: https://www.amajordifference.com/
- Bach flower essences:
  https://www.bachremedies.com/en-ca/
- Chromotherapy:
  Color Medicine by Charles Klotsche
- Facial Reflexology:
  https://mindbodybeautyinstitute.com/

About the Author

Lindsey Carter, LCSW, is a former mental health therapist, Army veteran, and self-proclaimed paradigm shifter renowned for her ability to identify where we're playing too small and have boxed ourselves in.

By sharing her thoughts on the original blueprint for humanity, she sparks a deep remembrance of who we are and what we're capable of.

Influenced by her battles with Lyme Disease and trauma, Carter's work invites us to expand our perspective on the way we relate to our minds and bodies, and inspires us to reconnect to our humanity.

Learn more at wildhearthuman.com